Anthony Hecht

American University Studies

Series XXIV
American Literature

Vol. 7

PETER LANG
New York • Bern • Frankfurt am Main • Paris

Norman German

Anthony Hecht

PETER LANG
New York • Bern • Frankfurt am Main • Paris

Library of Congress Cataloging-in-Publication Data

German, Norman
    Anthony Hecht / Norman German.
        p. cm.—(American university studies. Series
XXIV, American literature ; vol. 7)
    Bibliography: p.
    Includes index.
    1. Hecht, Anthony, 1923-   — Criticism and
interpretation.   I. Title.   II. Series.
PS3558.E28Z68   1989   811'.54—dc19   88-23835
ISBN 0-8204-0840-9   CIP
ISSN 0895-0512

CIP-Titelaufnahme der Deutschen Bibliothek

German, Norman:
Anthony Hecht / Norman German. — New
York; Bern; Frankfurt am Main; Paris: Lang,
1988.
    (American University Studies: Ser. 24,
    American Literature; Vol. 7)
    ISBN 0-8204-0840-9

NE: American University Studies / 24

© Peter Lang Publishing, Inc., New York 1989

Printed by Weihert-Druck GmbH, Darmstadt, West Germany

for Frank
who started all this

CONTENTS

ACKNOWLEDGMENTS

Atheneum-Macmillan and the Oxford University Press have been generous in allowing me to quote liberally from the poems of Anthony Hecht, who in turn has been most gracious in his correspondence with me.

For their sturdy comments and advice, I am deeply indebted to Jack Bedell, Barbara Cicardo, Frank Gaik, and R. S. Gwynn. A special thanks to Richard Cox and to Jayne Bordelon and LAZERSET, INC., for their care and patience in helping prepare the manuscript.

Shortened Notations

Stones	*A Summoning of Stones*
Hours	*The Hard Hours*
Shadows	*Millions of Strange Shadows*
Vespers	*The Venetian Vespers*

INTRODUCTION

Preliminaries

Always with trepidation I approach the moral verse of Anthony Hecht. I turn from the poems astonished and vulnerable, compelled to make myself and the world better. For despite a determinism that seems finally to have set up housekeeping in the sanctum sanctorum of our innermost selves, all of us wish the world were subject to change by our undetermined wills. The central tension of Hecht's philosophy betrays that he wants it both ways: utterly free beings perambulating in a strictly causal universe. John Crowe Ransom, Hecht's mentor at Kenyon College in the mid-forties, wrote a poem called "Survey of Literature" which opens, "In all the good Greek of Plato / I lack my roast beef and potato." Hecht certainly admits spirit, yet throughout his verse, which often reads like a mystic organizing his experience according to logical systems, he gives the impression of a man who wants to have his Plato and eat his potato, too.

Hecht's espousal of the world's deterministic heart in a number of poems, such as "The Gardens of the Villa d'Este" and "As Plato Said," does not, for him at least, preclude a mysterious and awful Being with a dash of whim, like the Old Testament Yahweh, who is exempt from the laws of His creation. It is not surprising to find Hecht worshiping at the body's altar in a poem like "The Ghost in the Martini," about-facing in the next poem, and kowtowing to some unifying transcendent principle such as he acknowledges in "'Gladness of the Best.'" Other poems testify to the dialectical workings of Hecht's mind: "Swan Dive," with its alternating stasis and flux; "Alceste in the Wilderness," in which man's animal and social natures compete; and "La Condition Botanique," whose domesticated jungle perches uncomfortably between utterly wild nature and the inimical industrialism despised by Ransom.

The poems, that is, present a man impaled on the horns of the dualistic dilemma. And there thriving.

Biographical

Anthony Evan Hecht was born January 16, 1923, in New York City to Melvyn Hahlo Hecht, a businessman, and Dorothea (Holzman) Hecht. In his mythopoeic, quasi-autobiographical essay "Masters of Unpleasantness," Hecht recalls that he was "conspicuous for mediocrity" throughout his school years. His "worried parents" sent him to the Pratt Institute for two days of aptitude testing and tried to keep from him "the bleakness of the findings." Finally succumbing to his exceptional proddings, they confessed that "Pratt had said decisively that [he] had no aptitudes whatever. And this only confirmed a fairly uniform opinion of teachers and family with which [the boy] was painfully obliged to agree."[1]

Wondering how he got "into this racket" of poetry, Hecht tells the story of misunderstanding a childhood song:

> My body lies over the ocean,
> My body lies over the sea,

> My body lies over the ocean,
>
> O bring back my body to me.

The surrealistic image engendered metaphysical speculations in the "thoughtful child" (contradicting the mediocre-child story): "What was my body doing out there, anyway? Was it getting wet? And where was *I* in the meantime?" The adult Hecht concluded nevertheless that "though all the germs of a mystic experience were present, they did not consolidate into any interest in poetry, or anything else, for that matter," thus leaving his reader entertained, but no more enlightened concerning his initiation into "this racket" than before.

However the seed was planted, it germinated during his freshman year at college. His parents' reaction to his poetic intentions? "Had I said that I'd settled upon a career of burglary, they might have been pained but would at least have credited me with a cool, prudential instinct for survival." As it was, they called in their only literary friend, the actual Dr. Seuss (Ted Geisel), who recommended to the seventeen-year-old that before launching a career as poet he should read "the life of Joseph Pulitzer." Fearing something "gravely discouraging" in the biography, Hecht "resolved quite firmly never to read it, and I never have. This policy seems to have served me well, and I commend it unreservedly to all young poets."

After receiving his B.A. from Bard College, Annandale-on-Hudson, New York, in 1944, Hecht was inducted into the U.S. Army and served three years as an infantry rifleman in Western Europe and Japan, thereafter serving temporary duty with the Counter-Intelligence Corps. In Czechoslovakia and Germany, "his unit discovered mass graves filled with thousands of charred bodies. He was one of the soldiers who liberated Flossenburg, an annex to the Buchenwald concentration camp."[2] Hecht earned the M.A. from Columbia University in 1950 and is the recipient of honorary doctorates from Bard and Georgetown University.

Upon Hecht's return to the States, fellow soldier Robie Macauley, future editor of the *Kenyon Review*, encouraged him to apply for admission on the GI bill to Kenyon College where John Crowe Ransom was teaching. Hecht's impressions of that time and of Ransom's personality are reported with a combination of awe and self-mocking humor in a 1980 *American Scholar* essay.[3] At Kenyon he was "assimilated into a hieratic tradition, a select branch in the great taxonomic structure of the modern intellect, in which we were the direct and undisputed heirs not only of Mr. Ransom himself but of all our distinguished predecessors who were his former pupils," among them Robert Lowell, Allen Tate, Cleanth Brooks, and Robert Penn Warren. "The responsibility of following in so august a procession we regarded as a difficult historic burden, just sufficiently mitigated by our private sense of being among 'the anointed.'" "We were all either secret or confessed poets—as well, of course, as being close readers, exegetes, speculative aestheticians, and literary ontologists."

Hecht's admiration of Ransom as a teacher is undiluted, his solicitous concern for him almost brotherly: "As part of his smoking paraphernalia Mr. Ransom always carried with him in his right-hand trouser pocket a thick clutch, a sort of beaver dam, of strike-anywhere kitchen matches. It seemed to me that some grace or special providence never allowed these matches to ignite as they constantly rubbed against one another in that pocket. But I was often anxious in his behalf." The "particular notions or propositions" Hecht learned from the distinguished New Critic have blurred with time, he claims. What remain are "a posture of the mind and spirit, a humanity and courtesy, a manly considerateness that inhabited [Ransom's] work as it did his person."

Hecht's marriage to Patricia Harris in 1954 produced his sons Jason and Adam, who are celebrated in poems in *The Hard Hours*. On June 12, 1971, Hecht married Helen D'Alessandro. Their meeting and falling in love is allegorized in "Peripeteia," from *Millions of Strange Shadows*. In a 1986 *Publishers Weekly* interview, Hecht says they "first met many years ago" at Smith College. "Many years later," they encountered each other at a dinner party celebrating Mona Van Duyn's National Book Award. Four days after their first date, on their second date, Hecht proposed and they were married three months after the dinner party. Past managing editor of Walker and Company and author of *Cold Cuisine* and *Cuisine for All Seasons*, Helen is the dedicatee of *Millions of Strange Shadows* and *The Venetian Vespers*, their son Evan of Hecht's collection of essays, *Obbligati*.[4]

Hecht has taught at Kenyon, State University of Iowa, New York University, Smith, and Bard. From 1967 to 1982, he was John H. Deane Professor of Poetry and Rhetoric at the University of Rochester. He spent visiting lecturer interims at Washington University in 1971, Harvard in 1973, and Yale in 1977. From 1982 to 1984 Hecht was poetry consultant to the Library of Congress. He currently teaches at Georgetown University.

His many major awards and honors include a Prix de Rome fellowship, 1951; Guggenheim fellowships, 1954, 1959; a *Hudson Review* fellowship, 1958; Ford Foundation fellowships, 1960, 1968; Pulitzer Prize in poetry, 1968, for *The Hard Hours*; and an Academy of American Poets fellowship, 1969. Hecht was a Fulbright professor in Brazil in 1971, and in 1983 was made a trustee of the American Academy in Rome.

The Books

Perhaps the informing thread running through all of Hecht's poems is the nagging question voiced in "A Poem for Julia," from *A Summoning of Stones*: "But in our fallen state . . . / What do we know of lasting since the fall?" A quarter century later, his pearls still solidify around the same irritation. The title poem of *The Venetian Vespers* asks, "What is our happiest, most cherished dream / Of paradise? Not harps and fugues and feathers / But rather arrested action, an escape / From time, from history, from evolution / Into the blessèd stasis of a painting. . . ." This fall, for Hecht, is not so much a moral lapse as a decline of perception, especially the perception of a child, who internalizes the world's images almost unmediated. His percepts are as uncontaminated by concepts as they will ever be. Recapturing this lost perception, and reanimating the world thereby, forms a kind of holy quest for Hecht that leads him only rarely into a mysticism as cabalistic as Blake's or Yeats'.

About the first volume, *A Summoning of Stones* (1954), Donald Davie said, "There is no pretence that the ostensible subject exists for the poet except as a peg on which to hang the embroidered robe of style; and style, thus cut loose of any responsibilities towards what it offers to express, degenerates at once into virtuosity, frigid accomplishment."[5] The book is a document of pure joy blighted by a malignant speck sure to corrupt that joy: "the unbidden terror and bone hand / Of gracelessness" of the opening poem. It is a record as well of the poet as necromancer and his poems as necromancy to charm a degenerative world into stasis at the just-right moment, as the volume's epigraph intimates: ". . . to call the stones themselves to their ideal places, and enchant the very substance and skeleton of the world." The volume, too, gives the impression of a person attempting to formulate and voice the ineffable: "The heart is ramified with an old force / (Outlingering the blood, out of the sway / Of its own fleshy trap) that finds its source / Deep in the phosphorous waters of the bay, / Or in the wind, or pointing cedar tree, / Or its own ramified complexity."

Almost completely purged of the exhibitionistic tendency of the first book is *The Hard Hours* (1967), the 1968 Pulitzer Prize-winner. With a marked ascendance of theme over form, a message within a frame that does not call undue attention to itself, the volume's utterances about family and the individual's place in history clearly matter.[6] If there is no disavowal of the New Critical principle of aesthetic distance between poet and his "object," there is a notable departure from it and an occasional excursion into strict confession. Other poems, "Rites and Ceremonies" especially, remind the reader of the restraining, even civilizing, influence of form (in manners and religion) on the appetites and passions.

Millions of Strange Shadows (1977), exorcised of a Dark Night's demons, returns to the self-referential craft of the first volume, though its self-conscious ingenuity is less strutting. The book, in a variety of styles and forms (blank verse, a sestina, an unrhymed sonnet, odes, translations, even a surrealistic prose poem) shows Hecht at his widest range. Heavier poems about war and responsibility ("The Cost," "Black Boy in the Dark"), archetypal cruelty ("The Feast of Stephen"), and the evolution of self-directed hatred ("Green: An Epistle") are balanced by those concerning the poet's role ("'Dichtung und Wahrheit'"), the miracle of new love ("Peripeteia"), and some deft nature pieces. In a class apart is "'Gladness of the Best,'" a tour de force of seamless bonding between form and content. Spicing the collection are the academic sexuality of "Goliardic Song" and the darkly humorous

"Ghost in the Martini," both of which unleash the libido held at bay in the first volume's manicured gardens.[7]

Vernon Shetley has hit on something significant when he says of the title poem of *The Venetian Vespers* (1979), "This lengthy 'Gerontion' comprehensively renders the quality of self-loathing and pained consciousness it sets out to portray, but is perhaps not so successful in convincing us of the value of the undertaking. Dwelling at such lengths on neurotic states is not without its dangers, and it may be questioned whether this dissection of the 'gross, intestinal wormings of the brain' is wholly consistent with good imaginative hygiene."[8] While some of the poems do seem sensational ("The Deodand," "The Short End"), the sheer virtuosity of description redeems the poetry just as the world's extravagance saves the decadent persona of "The Venetian Vespers." In his 1982 essay "Masters of Unpleasantness," Hecht tells the story of a well-known fiction writer who exclaimed that "poetry is so much easier to write than fiction." Instead of retracting in self-righteous indignation, Hecht gave the matter some thought and explained in the essay, "While novelists must labor under the compulsion to *invent*, to create fictional personages, put them in provocative situations, contrive actions and reactions and eventualities, poets have more and more retreated into undisguised narcissism and documentary literalness until, as things now go, a poet may be congratulated for being truthful, candid or confessional, but he is rarely told that he is, nor is he expected to be, imaginative. Imagination these days seems to belong to the realm of prose."[9] Heresy? I think not. Clearly, we have not seen in recent years a storyteller like Frost, nor do we see one's wavy head topping the horizon. Yet the poems of *Vespers* were already practicing what their master later preached in the 1982 essay and are as different from those in *Shadows* as those in *Hours* are from those in *Stones*. Hecht seems now to be challenging himself to be "creative" in an old way so long ignored it looks new again. The long poems of his most recent volume read more like highly polished short stories than Browning *redivivus*.

Despite its frequent baroque reveling in nature's plenitude, noted by critics to the point of tedium, Hecht's oeuvre is contaminated by a heavy dross of pessimism. Especially in these latter years have articles appeared, some indited by the poet himself, with such foreboding titles as "Poet for a Dark Age" in which critics see Hecht as the literary scion of Thomas Hardy. Yet in his most recent periodical poems, Hecht seems to be kicked back and relaxing, enjoying again the ludic gymnastics of the inventive mind of *Stones*, not giving a damn who remarks his happy egotism: "It's true / I'm no Bob Dylan, but I've more than one / Electric fan who likes the things I do: / Putting some English on the words I've spun // And sent careening over stands of birch / To beat the local birds at their own game. . . ."[10]

Method

In the following four chapters, Hecht's four major books of poetry are surveyed chronologically. The poems within each volume are treated either in their rhetorical alignments or in thematic groupings. The reader will discover that the groupings are more gropings for an organizing structure for the study than exclusive or definitive thematic corrallings of the poems. Hecht's small canon has provided me the opportunity to dwell on each poem at length, so some of the commentary on the individual poems might have little bearing on the theme under which they are discussed. The liberal citations are intended to give the reader a fair sampling of each poem's "local texture," wherein resides its "tissue of meaning," which Ransom says cannot, in any case, be rendered in prose.[11]

I had come to my conclusions about Hecht's poems long before I had come to his collected critical commentary in *Obbligati*, but I sometimes resort to his words there to bolster my arguments here (surely a hazardous enterprise) because they seem to me to clarify some points about the poems and because, as Emerson says, in them I "recognize [my] own rejected thoughts" now come back to me "with a certain alienated majesty."

In "The Evolution of Ransom's Critical Theory: Image and Idea," an appraisal of the famous teacher's critical theories and their effects, Thomas Daniel Young says, "Now he would say a poem is an 'organism,' composed of head, heart, and feet. All these organs work together to produce a poem, each speaking in a different language, the head in an intellectual language, the heart in an affective language, and the feet in a rhythmical language."[12] Appropriating these designations, one might say the present study concentrates mostly on the poems' "logical structures," less on their affective accomplishments, and still less on their metrics, though on occasion I dwell on the rhyme patterns when they fuss for attention, as in "'Gladness of the Best.'"

I should confess here in the mudroom that some of the more intractable poems I stretched to the breaking point on the rack of my critical apparatus, this in hopes that the strain on the verse might wrench free the surplus meaning they seemed unwilling to relinquish of their own accord. I claim no arcane connection with the critical muse. For any errors in judgment or taste, I am fully responsible, yet ask the reader to understand that the momentary lapse was probably due to my being switched across the eye and momentarily blinded by the whiplash of a Hechtian delayed apostrophic vocative embedded in a patch of ponderous dystax.

CHAPTER ONE

A Summoning of Stones

"Man's Painful Doubleness"

A Summoning of Stones concerns what "At the Frick" calls "man's painful doubleness," his physical and spiritual natures which cause him to lead lives alternately base and sublime. Yet the poems that first delineate this theme—"At the Frick," "The Place of Pain in the Universe," and "Harangue"—Hecht chose to leave out of *The Hard Hours*, the Pulitzer Prize-winning book at the back of which are gathered the poems he felt were worth salvaging.[1]

What one gets in that last section of *Hours* are highly crafted poems distanced by their irony and wit from the emotional pain and intellectual toil which generated what John Crowe Ransom would call their "loose logical structure." What one misses is the chance to view a philosophic mind wrestling with the most pressing of problems, in the orphaned poems finding expression in nothing less than a theodicy, and forcing them into artistic form. I belabor this point because *Stones* has been out of print for some time and the poems I will discuss first are not easily accessible.

The several poems in *Stones* about "man's painful doubleness" have as gnawing central concern the question formulated in "A Poem for Julia": "What do we know of lasting since the fall?" Another common denominator is their use of paintings as meditative objects. The epistemological question finds no comfortable solution for the poet until his third volume, *Millions of Strange Shadows*, and the theme is

conspicuously abandoned in *The Venetian Vespers*. The interest in paintings—
refinement of their use in the poems and especially translation of their graphic
strategies into rhetorical ones—continues to the present.

"A Poem for Julia" can be profitably studied as the prototype of the meditative
poem Hecht would alter to his purpose over the next three decades. Generally, the
meditative poems use art objects to launch the persona's lyrical, quasi-philosophi-
cal musings. In *A Summoning of Stones*, the poems which adhere to this pattern—
"The Place of Pain in the Universe," "At the Frick," and the two garden poems—
seem reluctant to touch upon the poet's personal life. Later, in *The Hard Hours,* but
more especially in *Millions of Strange Shadows*, Hecht attaches personal references to the poem's end, giving the poem's first part a homiletic quality. The
technique reaches its best expression in "A Birthday Poem" and "Going the
Rounds," both from *Shadows*, though the traces of the prototypical structure are
much subdued in the latter poem.[2]

"A Poem for Julia" never gets to the announced subject of its title. Though a
poem *for* someone is not necessarily *about* someone, the inertia of "A Poem for
Julia" leans in the direction of direct address or some overt expression of Julia's
beauty until stanza five, at which point the persona seems to change his mind, for
reasons I will attempt to outline.

The rhetorical structure of the poem's first two stanzas is one Hecht will rely on
many times in future poems where, however, that structure is not so obviously
commented on as in the present poem. Ultimately focusing on a madonna who sat
for Hans Memling, stanza one describes a painting by the fifteenth-century Flemish
artist. Memling's

... accomplished busy hand
Rendered this wimpled lady in such white
Untinted beauty, that she seems to stand
Even as gently to our present gaze
As she had stood there in her breathing days.

This stanza pays usual homage to the immortalizing quality of art, the stanza's final line recalling the now dead "hand of 'almost flawless skin'" of its first line. The opening of stanza two, "Seeing this painting, I am put in mind," is the transitional hook. In later poems, Hecht avoids this obvious shift from meditative object to the poem's actual but belated subject by resorting to metaphor, as in "A Birthday Poem," where, after dwelling on paintings by Mantegna, Holbein, and the Flemish masters, he says, "It's when we come to shift the gears of tense / That suddenly we note / A curious excitement of the heart. . . ."

In "A Poem for Julia," the transition delays rather than advances. The painting in stanza one reminds the persona of other paintings. Stanza two tells the reader that "art and history" record ugliness and moral beauty as well as physical beauty, indifferently immortalizing them so that a "pimpled, chinless shepherd" by accident or fate achieves "astonishing renown" by being associated in paintings with Magi adoring the Christ child and Mother, who "Ate of her portion with a flawless hand." The "'*almost* flawless skin'" of Memling's physically beautiful madonna is contrasted with the "flawless hand" of an anonymous Italian painter's morally beautiful Virgin Mother.

Stanza three about-faces, relating an anecdote about the judgmental aspect of

art. After a "foul-minded clergyman" said the *Last Judgment* was "a lewd and most
indecent show / Of nakedness," Michelangelo "promptly drew his face / Horribly
gripped, his face a fist of pain, / Amongst those fixed in God's eternal wrath. . . ."
The last part of the stanza records Pope Paul's reply to the complaint of "the fool."

"Had art set you on Purgatory's Mount
Then had I done my utmost for your hope,
But Hell's fierce immolation takes no count
Of offices and prayers, for as you know,
From that place *nulla est redemptio*."

In stanza four, "history tells the tale" of ermined ambassadors who went to Prague
"to seek avoidances of future wars," only to be the victims of a courtier-wit's
scatological practical joke.

. . . he pushed them through
The open-standing window, whence they fell,
Oh, in a manner worthy to be sung,
Full thirty feet into a pile of dung.

Having delivered two exempla each of art's and history's ability to hold up individuals for eternal praise, condemnation, or ridicule, the persona moves closer home in stanza five to poetry's similar taxidermic effect.

> How many poets, with profoundest breath,
> Have set their ladies up to spite the worm,
> So that pale mistress or high-busted bawd
> Could smile and spit into the eye of death
> And dance into our midst all fleshed and firm
> Despite she was most perishably flawed?

The persona's mocking tone in the "profoundest breath" that poets use in paying reverence to their loves' beauty suggests that he is unwilling to subject his art to or publish Julia's beauty for the cynical inspection of readers.

The poem has progressed from the "'almost flawless skin'" of stanza one and "flawless hand" of two to the "perishably flawed" women of five. At this point, the persona realizes two things. One, that what is later worshiped is the art, not the woman. Two, that he does not wish to put Julia in the company of flawless or almost flawless women or especially poets' perishably flawed mistresses and high-busted bawds.

In a way, this is a high compliment, not to share her beauty with anyone else, not to publicize and thereby prostitute her special graces. As Donne would have it, "'Twere profanation of our joys / To tell the laity our love." Another good reason to keep Julia to himself is that he dislikes the cold, marmoreal effect of poetry which, unlike graphic art, cannot elicit voyeuristic lust:

> She lasts, but not in her own body's right,
>
> Nor do we love her for her endless poise.
>
> All of her beauty has become a part
>
> Of neighboring beauty, and what could excite
>
> High expectations among hopeful boys
>
> Now leaves her to the nunnery of art.

To commit his love to the sterile, albeit durable, "nunnery" of poetry seems blasphemous to the persona—that her memorial replica can achieve immortality while her actual beauty must decay.

The persona's meditation on perfection leads him astray in the final stanza to metaphysical worries and eventually to Hecht's most voluted mystical utterance. Understanding that only Adam and Eve knew such perfection as art tries to achieve, the persona asks what endures since the fall.

> Adam and Eve knew such perfection once,
>
> . . . .
>
> But in our fallen state where the blood hunts
>
> For blood, and rises at the hunting sound,
>
> What do we know of lasting since the fall?

The rising blood of war or lust represents flux, from which the persona desires escape into permanence, the quest that determines the tenor of nearly every poem in *A Summoning of Stones*.

> Who has not, in the oil and heat of youth,
>
> Thought of the flourishing of the almond tree,
>
> The grasshopper, and the failing of desire,
>
> And thought his tongue might pierce the secrecy
>
> Of the six-pointed starlight, and might choir
>
> A secret-voweled, unutterable truth?

Creeping doubt and fear contaminate ambitious youth, which thinks it can accomplish anything—even "choir" the Tetragrammaton, the Hebrew God's ineffable name rendered in Roman alphabets as "YHWH" or "JHVH," which, without vowels, cannot be pronounced. The reference to Ecclesiastes suggests that youth's vain desires will turn to dust. The impenetrable secrecy of creation and God is emphasized. Stymied in his epistemological inquiry, frustrated by his inability to articulate in any usual way the force he feels, the persona resorts to riddling mysticism.

> The heart is ramified with an old force
>
> (Outlingering the blood, out of the sway

Of its own fleshy trap) that finds its source
Deep in the phosphorous waters of the bay,
Or in the wind, or pointing cedar tree,
Or its own ramified complexity.

The persona seeks the force that produces and yet transcends the flux of moving water, wind, and growing trees and that is exempt from "the thousand natural shocks that flesh is heir to." The statement about the dynamics of liquids is similar to Dylan Thomas's formulation, "The force that drives the water through the rocks / Drives my red blood."

The mystery of the force manifests itself in the architectonics of the heart. By this force, "the heart is ramified," strengthened, and also encouraged, given hope. Stripped of its modifiers, the sentence claims that the force "finds its source . . . in . . . waters . . . wind . . . or . . . tree." The same force that moves the heart, moves water and wind by the action and reaction of cold and hot, shapes the tree by the pull and counterpull of gravity and light, and gives each element (water, wind, trees) direction. The pervasive force should also direct both the literal and figurative heart.

The passage's ultimate paradox, the more intriguing because a Möbius strip-like tautology, is that "The heart is ramified with an old force . . . that finds its source . . . in . . . its own ramified complexity." The heart is ramified (strengthened) by its own ramifications (branchings, from Latin *ramus*, branch) or network of arteries and chambers. Pure Emerson, the statement claims that the creative force of nature is both transcendent and immanent.

In three sentences of the poem's last stanza, the poet leaps from casual observances about art to a disquisition on the nature of perfection to arcane metaphysical utterances. A reader might quiz himself dizzy concerning the relation of all this to the Julia of the title. If Hecht was suffering from the anxiety of influence, he may have wanted not only to work within the poetic tradition of praising one's beloved but to rewrite or update the rules of that tradition in order competitively to best it.

The key, I think, is in the parenthetical comment, "(Outlingering the blood, out of the sway / Of its own fleshy trap)," that interrupts the last sentence. The force that moves water, wind, and trees "outlinger[s]," outlasts, "the blood" of war or passion. The force is "out of the sway / of its [the blood's] own fleshy trap," the valves of the heart which stop, pool, and help propel the life-force of the body. In an extremely circuitous way, the poem is about immortalizing physical and moral beauty. If we add the mystical truth of the final stanza, we have the old Greek standbys of Goodness, Truth, and Beauty. And, on this earth, as Keats reminds us, "Beauty is truth, truth beauty," and that is all we need to know.

Rather than committing Julia to "the nunnery of art," the persona wishes to give her a truly immortal gift, transcendental knowledge. The attempt at any immortality imparted by art is based on what Sir Thomas Browne called "a fallacy in duration," a phrase that Hecht cites to similar ends in his essay "Houses as Metaphors: The Poetry of Architecture."[3] Instead of praising his beloved, the persona resorts to gift-giving, another common poetical convention. Here, the poet offers the beauty of Truth. If he can pull it off, he outdoes even Shakespeare, whose love is immortal only as long as "men can breath, or eyes can see" to read his sonnet, which though a nice sentiment is not, after all, forever.

A shorter meditation, "At the Frick" opens abruptly with a factual statement uncharacteristic of Hecht's typically florid diction and complicating syntax: "Before a grotto of blue-tinted rock / Master Bellini has set down St. Francis." The introduction is appropriately general, as if revealing the persona's first impression after stepping up to Bellini's *St. Francis in Ecstasy* in New York's Frick collection. Attention is then paid to details, the imaginative mind of the persona spinning metaphors out of the images he sees.

> A light split through the Apennines to lock,
> Counter, and splice man's painful doubleness,
> Else he could weakly couple at the belt
> His kite-mind to his cloven nether parts
> That seek to dance their independent dances.

The speaker thinks of the rope of the Franciscans as dividing man in two, his animal self ("cloven nether parts") below the belt and his rational self ("kite-mind") above. The conflict caused by this dual nature finds traditional expression in the Apollonian and Dionysian tensions of classical mythology and in the troubles of Plato's charioteer as he tries to coordinate the horses of spirit and appetite seeking "to dance their independent dances."

The body, however, is not totally denigrated. "Lock" and "splice" indicate that man's task is to balance his kite-mind and cloven nether parts. A spirit that soars too high is as ineffectual as a body that grovels in its animality. Body, then, should serve as ballast for spirit.

In the second stanza, the persona focuses on the animal minutiae scattered throughout the painting.

> Fisher of birds and lepers, lost in thought,
> Darkly emblazoned, where the oblivious mule
> Champs at the grasses and the sunset rusts
> The hilltop fortress, where the painter set
> Heron and rabbit, it was here he caught
> Holiness that came swimming like a school
> Of silver fishes to outflash his lusts.

The imagery summarizes man's dichotomous nature. The animal kingdom—represented by the birds, mule, heron, rabbit, and fishes—opposes the heavenly kingdom towards which St. Francis aspires by being a Christian fisher not only of ordinary men, but also of "birds and lepers." The animals emphasize man's "doubleness" of gender, male and female, a painful duality of identity represented in Plato's etiological myth of the two sexes being split by the Demiurge from one spherical being. Additionally, it is hard not to associate the mule, sterile hybrid of what may be termed a genetically weak coupling, with the celibate St. Francis.

St. Francis has characteristics of all the animals. Like the rabbit, he burrows, lives in a grotto; like the mule, he is "sterile," lives a celibate life; like the birds associated with him, his spirit soars. His intense spirituality derives its power from a controlled animality. Though he is sterile like the mule, he is not "oblivious"; though he retains the sexual energy of the rabbit, he stores rather than expends it, which sublimation, in part, causes his spirit to soar, causes his ecstasy.

According to H. W. Janson, in *St. Francis in Ecstasy* the saint is a natural part of the landscape.

> The saint is here so small in comparison to the setting that he seems almost incidental, yet his mystic rapture before the beauty of the visible world sets our own response to the view that is spread out before us, ample and intimate at the same time. He has left his wooden pattens behind and stands barefoot on holy ground, like Moses in the Lord's presence.[4]

St. Francis has, in the painting, left a *closed* book on his table and stepped out to meet nature open-armed. Barefoot, he is linked to the earth, though his eyes gaze heavenward. He stands comfortably set in his duality, like the bubble in a carpenter's level. The poem depicts the rope-belt not so much as pinching him in two as splicing the worldly to the divine, his ecstasy caused by communion with both nature and God.

The saint's and, by extension, all men's isolate and social selves are symbolized in the school of fishes and the fortress, which is set apart from the hermit "lost in thought," though in visiting the lepers he takes part in a community of pariahs. Man's good-evil tensions are embedded in the fortress, with its martial implications, and in the understated mention of the saint's lust. Throughout the stanza, the spiritual is the privileged term in man's material-spiritual nature, as borne out in the decaying lepers and rusting fortress. To heighten these contrasts, Hecht exaggerates the "light split through the Apennines" in Bellini's actual painting. Finally, "darkly emblazoned" clinches, oxymoronically, man's linked but opposed doubleness.

The speaker's reflection culminates in a *memento mori* last stanza.

> Now I have seen those mountains, and have seen
> The fawn go frozen on the road with fear
> Of the careening autobus, the sheen
> Of its dilated eyes flash in its head
> Like glass reflectors, and have seen the trees
> As green as ever where their branches thresh
> The warm Italian winds of one more year
> Since that great instant. The painter's dead
> Who brought the Doge and nobles to the knees
> Of the wind's brother Francis in the flesh.

Here, the "I" enters the poem and history and realizes that, like saint and painter, he will die. That nature and art endure provides little solace to the persona. Adding to the speaker's anxiety is the fact that machinery threatens the normal life cycle of nature. Just as St. Francis has a skull on his desk (in painting, not poem), the speaker has an updated Nemesis, the autobus, a potent reminder that his life, like the fawn's, could be annihilated at any moment.

The tripartite division of the poem is revelatory, each stanza representing a cultural epoch. The poem seems to argue that during the Middle Ages, a premium was put on Goodness, personified by St. Francis; in the Renaissance, on Beauty, personified by Bellini; in the modern era, one might expect Truth to be embodied in the speaker, yet the impersonal and destructive technology is ascendant, the persona obliquely associated with the fawn "frozen on the road with fear" of this technological juggernaut. Further, in the "glass reflector" image of the fawn's eyes, there is a shift from anthropomorphism to technomorphism, an alienation of man from the majestic landscapes of Bellini's painting, with an accompanying impotence to effect change in the world, in contrast with the ability of St. Francis and Bellini to bring nobles to their knees. Any such "great instant" of influence is impossible in the current technocratic dispensation.

The poem's final sentence reiterates man's painful doubleness. The "flesh" and "wind" represent earth-bound body and ethereal spirit. A modern irony concludes the poem: art pays homage to its artificer by outliving and immortalizing him; machinery victimizes its creator.

If "At the Frick" gives the cause of pain as man's "doubleness," "The Place of Pain in the Universe" gives, not pain's expected philosophical "place," the reason for its existence, but its physical locus.

> Mixture of chloroform and oil of cloves
> Swabbed with a wadded toothpick on the gums
> Grants us its peace by slackening the thread

> Of rich embroidered nerve spun in the head,
>
> And to the weak and wretched jaw it comes
>
> Lighter than manna and in sweeter loaves.

A "nerve . . . in the head" is the literal place of pain. Unlike "At the Frick," this poem values the life of the flesh, at least when the body is not distressed. Whereas "At the Frick" begins with St. Francis and Bellini, "The Place of Pain in the Universe" waits until its second stanza to broach a saint and painting-as-meditative-object, in this case actually an engraving.

> An old engraving pictures St. Jerome
>
> Studying at his table, where a skull,
>
> Crowned with a candle, streams cold tears of wax
>
> On its bone features for the flesh it lacks,
>
> Yet its white complement of teeth is full
>
> While all its pain runs happily to loam.

Perhaps, this stanza claims, it is better to be flesh in pain, even with a toothache that calls for extraction, than a lifeless skull with a full set of smiling teeth, for to be painless is to be bodiless, when the flesh runs "happily to loam." The literally hot candle wax dripping down the skull's cheek produces figuratively "*cold* tears," unfeeling tears. The dialectical swing of desiring the world of the body (with the ambiguous benefits derived therefrom and the potential for pleasure or pain) and the world of the spirit causes the last stanza's tension, which is similar to that experienced by Ransom's "Equilibrists."

Observe there is no easy moral here.
Having received their diet from the skies
The teeth remain, although they cannot bite,
And to perform inspection beyond sight
The empty sockets famish for their eyes.
The pain is lifelike in that waxwork tear.

While our spiritual side desires the food of heaven, needing the proper eyes to see and ears to hear, and desires insight "to perform inspection beyond sight," the body has its own hungers so that even after death its "empty sockets famish for their eyes." What is hard, skull and teeth, endures; what is tender, eyes and nerves, dies. Though returning to the life of the body would bring pleasure *and* pain, the choice here seems to be for the body.

The persona's questioning stance in "At the Frick" and "The Place of Pain in the Universe" is thinly disguised truculence at an allegedly benevolent Creator. For the persona, it seems not enough to say that pain is limited in duration and intensity. If pain were insignificant, why couldn't God have dispensed with it altogether? The skull questions, but by itself cannot find answers.

"Discourse Concerning Temptation" confirms the ambiguous nature of the world. "The place is neither Paradise nor Hell, / But of their divers attributes a blend: / It is man's brief and natural estate." So ends the poem which, with dozens of others in his canon, bears out the fact that something in Hecht doesn't trust the world. Earth may still be "the right place for love," but, hedging on Frost's optimism, Hecht might say, "I don't know where it's likely to go better *or worse*." "Discourse Concerning Temptation" may in fact be termed Hecht's celebration, with a tincture of pathos, of temptation's agent, the world's luxuriance. Doubtless, a seminal concept in Hecht's philosophical verse is luxury and its synonyms and etymological variants (*e.g.*, luxurious, excess, extravagance).

Performing the same function as St. Francis and St. Jerome in the previously discussed poems is the figure in the middle two stanzas of "Concerning Temptation," "a gentleman of severest taste / Who won from wickedness by consummate strife / A sensibility suitable to his chaste / Formula."

> . . . He found the world too lavish.
> Temptation was his constant, intimate foe,
> Constantly to be overcome by force, and so
> His formula (fearing lest the world ravish
> His senses) applied the rigors of art to life.

The man's asceticism causes psychological distress manifesting itself in an auto-induced Dantean punishment.

But in recurrent dreams saw himself dead,

Mourned by chrysanthemums that walked about,

Each bending over him its massive head

And weeping on him such sweet tender tears

That as each drop spattered upon his limbs

Green plant life blossomed in that place.

Just as Dante's suicides were turned into thorny trees for destroying their bodies, the luxuriance that Hecht's gentleman eschews haunts him in his Freudian dream-work. Sexual denial conjures forth the sensual imagery of pear and snake, here the fer-de-lance:

The problem is not simple. In Guadeloupe

The fer-de-lance displays his ugly trait

Deep in the sweaty undergrowth where droop

Pears of a kind not tasted, where depend

Strange apples, in the shade of *Les Mamelles*.

The place is neither Paradise nor Hell,

But of their divers attributes a blend:

It is man's brief and natural estate.

"The problem is not simple," and the problem is how to appreciate, even revel in, the world's splendor, when succumbing to it can bring disastrous consequences. Populated by snakes, the world is not Hell; hanging with apples, it is no Eden. It is "a blend" of both. The poem simultaneously celebrates and laments the nature of the world, and not without humor. Whereas the gentleman applies "the rigors of art to life" and wishes temptation would leave him be, the poem argues that the rigors of life (including erections) are better than the rigors of death (*rigor mortis*). There is a Goldilocks philosophy here that the world is just right. It is too bad it is brief, but it seems good that it is man's "natural estate," the poem's final word claiming that, while on earth, man is king of all he surveys.

Though I do not wish to make much of this, Hecht sometimes falls into redundancies because of the "tensions of composition," as Ransom says, stemming from a poet's working his meaning into rhythm and rhyme, so that not just often, but probably always "the meter coming in [drives] some of the logic out."[5] "Discourse Concerning Temptation" opens, "Though learned men have been at some dispute / Touching the taste and color, nature, name / And properties of the Original Fruit. . . ." The redundancy of "properties" is readily apparent: "taste and color" are both "properties" of the fruit. At the earliest point in his career, Hecht, under Ransom's tutelage at Kenyon, must have had a heightened awareness of the inherent problems of formal verse. Nonetheless, he chose to hazard its strictures in hopes of its special kinds of profits.[6]

"Alceste in the Wilderness" portrays a man caught between Paradise and Hell, that is, trapped in a world where society's preposterous extravagances and accoutrements contrast nature's unbuffered realities. Thematically, it is the crucial poem in *A Summoning of Stones*, since it resolves the book's tensions between matter and spirit by giving its protagonist over to his alternating preferences, emblematic of man's dialectical disposition. Neither Paradise nor Hell, the world does seem to resemble Purgatory, his frustrations attest.

The poem, a sequel to *The Misanthrope*, imagines Alceste after his disavowal of society. In Africa, where he has fled, Alceste becomes sated with the horror of the animal world: gnats, bees, ants, screaming birds, the corpse of a monkey.

> Force of the sun had split the bluish skin,
> Which, by their questioning and entering in,
> A swarm of bees had been concerned to sweeten.

> He could distill no essence out of this.
> That yellow majesty and molten light
> Should bless this carcass with a sticky kiss
> Argued a brute and filthy emphasis.

The monkey that has died alone in the wilderness suggests Célimène's harsh words to Alceste, "None but yourself shall make a monkey of you" (II.i.67). The corpse as beehive recalls both *Hamlet* (II.ii.176-82) and Judges 14.8. Hamlet's unfinished comment on honesty, also Alceste's major concern, is "Aye, sir, to be honest, as this world goes, is to be one man picked out of ten thousand. . . . For if the sun breed maggots in a dead dog, being a god kissing carrion—Have you a daughter?" (The spontaneous generation of maggots was a common belief in the seventeenth century.) In Judges, a young lion Samson has killed contains "a swarm of bees and honey in [its] carcase [*sic*]. . . ."

Even in the wilds of Africa, Alceste cannot escape his social self, reminded as he is of the human sexual dance in the birds' synesthetic mating cries:

> Evening is clogged with gnats as the light fails,
> And branches bloom with gold and copper screams
> Of birds with figured and sought-after tails
> To plume a lady's gear. . . .

Set in Africa, the poem resembles *Heart of Darkness*, in which Marlow goes into a jungle to search for Kurtz, in whose character he expects to find a clue to the evil around him. In both works, the "heart of darkness" is the jungle and man's dark, animalistic core.

Society's rapacity, seen in its exploitation of animals for the embellishment of its own barely disguised mating rituals, is derived from nature's rapacity. Alceste's snuffbox, too, betokens the society he has abandoned but subconsciously longs for.

> A little snuffbox whereon Daphnis sings
> In pale enamels, touching love's defeat,
> Calls up the color of her underthings. . . .

Because Daphnis was punished by Aphrodite for refusing the love of women,

Alceste's exile can be seen as a purgation.

Throughout the poem, the stark colors of nature jangle Alceste's nerves. The birds have "gold and copper screams"; the dead monkey has "bluish skin" and "white" fingernails; bees are working to store in the carcass their honey of "yellow majesty." The colors and decay of the monkey sicken Alceste, especially when he sees "How terribly the thing looked like [his friend] Philinte." Alceste begins to see at least one of society's virtues, its ability to buffer the solitariness of death in nature. Contrasting these monochromes are the muted or particolored objects of civilization: the "underthings" of Célimène and the "pale enamels" of the snuffbox. Despite its brilliant colors, Africa is still the Dark Continent. Already, the variegated colors of Versailles pull Alceste homeward.

> Before the bees have diagrammed their comb
> Within the skull, before summer has cracked
> The back of Daphnis, naked, polychrome,
> Versailles shall see the tempered exile home,
> Peruked and stately for the final act.

Given the options of the jungles of Africa with isolated death and the jungle of society with companionship, Alceste chooses the latter as the lesser of evils. According to the poem's logic, Alceste's return to society is as predictable as his dissatisfaction with society's polychromatics, too-subtle nuances, and mincing affectations. Misanthrope that he is, despiser of social hypocrisies, Alceste is no feral man either. In the play, Philinte warns Alceste,

> Yes, man's a beastly creature; but must we then
> Abandon the society of men? (V.i.79-80)

From corruption can issue something sweet, like honey in the monkey or in the biblical lion, or from a decadent society an honest and pure Eliante.

In "Alceste in the Wilderness," the misanthrope examines the "*small corpse* of a monkey" and its "*filthy* emphasis." In the poem that follows it, "Harangue," a coroner performs an autopsy on the "*long corpus* of society, / Divining *filthy* dreams it had in life." Related by more than diction, both poems have personae with dialectical minds and actions. Alceste feels the alternating attractions of community and solitude. In "Harangue," the persona's mystical and empirical selves spar, mysticism finally giving empiricism a thorough thrashing. However tell-tale the piece is concerning his philosophy, Hecht chose not to include the poem in *The Hard Hours*, perhaps because, as he explained in a letter to the author, "The title is a sort of embarrassed confession that I thought the poem too doctrinaire, too dependent upon the poetic theories of John Crowe Ransom."[7]

The guardedly optimistic persona tries his mysticism against the chill reason of the nihilistic, cynical coroner. As demonstrated by the italicized words below, Hecht's poem has striking syntactic and thematic parallels with Whitman's "When I Heard the Learn'd Astronomer." First, Whitman's complete poem:

When I heard the learn'd astronomer,

When the proofs, the *figures*, were ranged in

      columns before me,

When I was shown the charts and diagrams, to add,

      divide, and measure them

When I sitting heard the astronomer where he lectured

      with much applause in the lecture-room,

How soon unaccountable I became tired and sick,

Till rising and gliding out *I wander'd off by myself,*

In the mystical moist night-air, and from time to time,

Look'd up in perfect silence at the stars.

                (italics added)

Now Hecht's first stanza:

While, like a holy man, you kissed the sores

On the long corpus of society,

Divining filthy dreams it had in life,

The unbecoming seepings of its pores

Gathering meaning for you; *while* your knife

Picked at the chambers of the soul, the liver,

And you made *notes* to document the cluster

Of tumors breeding to satiety,

> With all bravado I could ably muster
> *I went for a sunny walk beside the river.*
>
> (italics added)

A when-then movement is the framework of both poems. Whereas Whitman's poem allows man's mystical leanings to win quickly and easily, Hecht's prolongs the speaker's thoughts on his mystical perceptions of nature. Hecht's scientist, inside an artificial environment, objectively and analytically observes life (ironically represented by a cadaver), while the subjectively and holistically oriented speaker wanders outside to experience nature and life synthetically. Hecht's persona carries on a debate with himself and with his coroner-friend, moving from inside to outside, while comparing and contrasting the scientific and mystical interpretations of life. The pattern of stanzas and dialogue forms a catechism, a thinly disguised polemic influenced by John Crowe Ransom's agrarian ideals and his notion of the different kinds of knowledge science and poetry impart.

In the second stanza, the speaker ambles outdoors, where he hears the "arrant warbling" of birds, whose song defies the scientist's findings and method of knowing (logical positivism):

> I can report no news about the birds.
> They are as ignorant as ever, sing
> In thoroughgoing boneheaded defiance
> Of all your findings. At a loss for words,

> They none the less repudiate your science.
> I have not the presumption to defend
> Such arrant warbling. My embarrassed logic
> Scored not at all against the treble ring
> Of music so unsuited to the tragic.
> They seemed to have no inkling of their end.

The ring is "treble" in its musical sense of light and happy. The speaker's gloomy mood and logic do not "score" against (seem insignificant in comparison to) the birds' song. Or, as the pun indicates, the scores do not match: logical and musical notations have no common ground for communication. Aesthetics wins out over reason.

In the next stanza, the mystic's burgeoning, animated world contrasts the scientist's restrictive, material world.

> Bird-witted? Doubtless, but their noisy creed
> Was seconded by inarticulate trees
> Whose wooden quiddity, erect and pliant,
> Sprouting luxurious beyond all need,
> Was by excess thus equally defiant,
> And all my thought, though diligent and tidy,
> Could not yet disestablish such a green
> Outburst. . . .

The speaker sees in nature an excess "beyond all need," redundant, not biologically necessary. There is no "logical" one-to-one correspondence between biological properties (birdsong, luxuriant foliage) and survival value. Nature's superabundance and sublimity seem to argue a life or presence beyond that which subsists on an elemental level because, at least to this persona, anything unnecessary is ontologically redundant. To employ more philosophical parlance, which the persona mocks, lush foliage is not essential to "tree-ness" any more than "arrant warbling" is to "bird-ness." The extraneous qualities therefore betoken for him a mysterious power in and behind them that, because they cannot contain it, spills over and manifests itself as exuberant excess. It is instructive to note here Ransom's words concerning what scientists do to images and objects when leeching from them their idea values. "It is . . . by abstraction that science destroys the image." An idea is an "image with its character beaten out of it."[8] "The icon is a particular. A particular is indefinable; that is, it exceeds definition. . . . A particular has too many properties, and too many values."[9]

This superfluous quality of nature that is uncapturable in scientific discourse has a counterpart in Hecht's poetics. Here and throughout Hecht's volumes can be found a deployment of *variation*, a poetic device characteristic of Old English versification. Birdsong, for example, within the span of nine lines, is called "thoroughgoing boneheaded defiance," "arrant warbling," "treble ring of music," and "noisy creed." The "equally defiant" lush foliage of trees is called "a green outburst," "rage of brilliance," and "green excess." The birds themselves are called "small musicians" and "tenant minstrelsy." Far from being uncalculated repetition, this technique of Hecht's seems concerned to salvage as much of an object's "texture" as possible.

Unlike the diffident hesitancy of previous personae in *Stones*, who shrink from pushing their line of reasoning to a conclusive statement ("Observe there is no easy moral here," in "The Place of Pain in the Universe"; "The problem is not simple," in "Discourse Concerning Temptation"), this one shows moral fortitude by saying, "Let us engage this difficulty." There is thus, in the volume's rhetorical organization, a progression of thought and clear gain of metaphysical confidence.

The speaker's engagement of the difficulty discovers that the difference between birds and trees on the one hand and man on the other lies in the latter's consciousness of death: "Yet man, / Outliving both the summer and its rage, / Numbers his days and knows them to be brief."

In the fifth stanza, impoverished reason and heady mysticism again do battle.

> "Man," as you often quote, "created death,"
> . . . .
> . . . And yet the flesh
> Is nothing but the substance that defied
> All reasoning; it is the green excess
> That tops the trees, and of the birds their song.

Man's hypersensitive flesh is brought into the argument and equated with arboreal and avian extrusions. Yet the persona is not cocky, by no means thinks himself victorious in the argument, for despite his drunken mysticism, personal death still haunts him in the bread-and-butter world.

> . . . It seems the dead,
> Though provender for the man-eating worms,
> Baffle us at the table and in bed
> With stark arithmetic and perfect reason.
>
> . . . .
>
> Not for themselves but for our mystery
> We watch the swift migrations of the season.

Discounting the cold rationalism of science, the persona is nonetheless affected by a more homely arithmetic. When a spouse dies, the simple arithmetic of $2-1=1$ at bed and breakfast reminds the surviving spouse with "perfect reason" that he or she is next. The persona's trouble with the practical application of his ethereal philosophy echoes Emerson's sublunary struggle with little Waldo's demise. Still, the last couplet of the stanza intimates, the cycle of seasons may promise human resurrection. The persona, however, seems dissatisfied with the weakly allegorical final stanza and resorts to another riverwalk to exit from the poem.

> Granted, there's reason for our reasoning.
> The tree becomes the instrument of passion;
> The bird is Death, the Violated Lady,
>
> . . . .
>
> Yet there is substance here beyond our talk,
> Stuff that defies the cynical romancer

> To whittle to his fantasy and fashion,
>
> And while you meditate upon your answer
>
> I shall go back to the river for a walk.

The persona certainly feels he has gained an edge on his overly cerebral opponent. The meaning behind the neo-Platonic phraseology of "*substance* here beyond our talk, / *Stuff* that defies the cynical romancer," while poking fun at the jargon of philosophical inquiry, bears the mark both of Whitmanesque mysticism,

> There is that in me—I do not know what it is. . . .
>
> . . . .
>
> . . . it is without name—it is a word unsaid.
>
> It is not in any dictionary, utterance, symbol,
>
> ("Song of Myself," Canto 50)

and the notion of words always meaning more than they are meant to mean. Thus, in Hecht's poem, the generative quality of words is joined to the extravagance of effusive birdsong and profuse foliage as proof of a reality beyond empirical perception. Both the technique and the sentiment reveal Ransom's influence.

The Law Of Sex

The mystery of sex and the law of sex show up as complementary forces in several of Hecht's poems. The epigraph of "As Plato Said," taken from Plutarch, affirms that the "public dances and other exercises of the young maidens naked" drew the young men "almost as necessarily by the attraction of love as a geometrical conclusion is drawn from the premises."

The young soldier who delivers the apostrophe to a particular girl constantly stresses that he is drawn, not so much by the specific maiden as by her abstract form, or "design" as he calls it, by the law of the urge within himself, and by a supranatural mystery whose prophetic message he reads in the turning daw above him.[10] That is, to fulfill its terms, the equation of the epigraph calls for something in her, something in him, and a mysterious catalytic force exterior to both.

> Although I do not know your name, although
> It was a silly dance you did with apple flowers
> Bunched in your hands after the racing games,
> My friends and I have spent these several hours
> Watching. Although I do not know your name. . . .

Protesting too much about her name, the youth in fact seems inordinately drawn to the one particular girl and resorts to omen-reading to explain her attractiveness.

This afternoon there was a giant daw

Turning above us—though I put no trust

In all these flying omens, being just

A plain man and warrior, like my friends—

Yet I am mastered by uncommon force

And made to think of you, although it blends

Not with my humor, or the businesses

Of Soldiering. . . .

He seeks an exterior explanation for his instrinsic obsession. The passive voice
captures his helplessness before this "law": "I am mastered by uncommon force /
And made to think of you." His two *idées fixes* are the girl and the daw.

But it is a compelling kind of law

Puts your design before me, even though

I put no faith or fancy in that daw

Turning above us. There is some rigor here,

More than in nature's daily masterpiece

That brings for us, with absolute and clear

Insistence, worms from their midnight soil,

Ungodly honk and trumpeting of geese

In the early morning, and at last the toil

Of soldiering. This is a simple code.

The young soldier claims it is more than instinct that draws him, something akin to a Platonic Idea of woman, her "design." Instinct calls worms from the ground, geese to migrate, and men to conquer foreign lands. Man is not exempt from the animals' instinctual movements and migrations, his territoriality driving him "at last [to] the toil / Of soldiering."

Along with the more insidious suggestion of *Lebensraum* is the raucous comparison of morning erections to animals: phallic "worms" drawn "from the midnight soil" and "ungodly honk and trumpeting of [long-necked] geese / In the early morning." The reader is prepared for the animals' phallic implications by a prefatory pun: "There's some rigor here, / More than in nature's daily masterpiece."

The youth is irritated by this other call than soldiering. Upon awakening from a domestic reverie concerning shepherding, farming, cooking, and spinning—sedentary and unsoldierly activities indeed—he resigns himself to the mysterious tyranny prophesied by the daw, again using a bawdy pun for erections.

> No. There is not a more unbending thing
> In nature. It is an order that shall find
> You out. . . .
> . . . .
> However we are governed, it shall draw
> Both of us to its own conclusions, though
> I do not even know you by your name.

This relentless yet undiscriminating law of sex finds similar expression in

"Divisions upon a Ground," retitled "Le Masseur de Ma Soeur" (playing on Wallace Stevens' "Le Monocle de Mon Oncle") in *The Hard Hours*. In "division" three, a male rebuts the female's charge that youth's follies mature into age's regrets by replying, "'Youth wants no emphasis, / But in extravagance of nature shows / A rigor more demanding than precise,'" "rigor" again concretizing the abstract, unwavering sexual law, what the poem later calls "the urgent lawless measure / Of love." The judicious use of "lawless" indicates that despite the "laws" of sex, its expression is often not law-abiding. The "extravagance of nature" reiterates the concept found in "Harangue," that nature has given man a sex drive the force and duration of which are many times what is necessary to propagate the species.

The poem, a series of arguments ("divisions" implies divisiveness) about sex (the "ground" for the arguments), concerns sublimation and socially acceptable and ritualized expressions of raw sexual energy. In division one, the narrator, apparently the brother of the "sister," immodestly disillusions her of her subconscious desires.

> My demoiselle, the cats are in the street,
> Making a shrill cantata to their kind,
> Accomplishing their furry, vigorous feat,
> And I observe you shiver at it. You
> Would rather have their little guts preserved
> In the sweet excellence of a string quartet.

Censoring, too, keeps people from directly confronting their sexuality, especially Americans, who are "deftly obscured from sin / By the Fig-Leaf Edition of Montaigne." The poem concludes:

> And who can cipher out, however shrewd,
> The Man-in-the-Moon's microcephalic grin?

The "code" of "As Plato Said" resurfaces as a "cipher" here. The image of the final couplet encapsulates the poem's theme, romantic love's mischievous ways of disguising brute sexuality.

"Samuel Sewall" recounts the reluctant courtship of the distinguished colonial judge who "gave not any figs" for the camouflaged rituals of sexuality.

> Samuel Sewall, in a world of wigs,
> Flouted opinion in his personal hair;
> For foppery he gave not any figs,
> But in his right and honor took the air.

The stanza alludes to a Colonel Townsend's wanting Sewall to wear a judge's wig in addition to his hood.[11] The fourth line plays on the "right honorable" Sewall's choice to go *au naturel*.

Thus in his naked style, though well attired,

He went forth in the city, or paid court

To Madam Winthrop, whom he much admired,

Most godly, but yet liberal with the port.

Sewall probably admired Winthrop for more than her godliness, her distinguished name perhaps being among her chief virtues. And if her drinking seemed excessive, his *Diary* reveals that he turned it to his romantic advantage by telling her that "her Kisses were . . . better than the best Canary" wine.[12] Despite his age, sixty-eight, he seems to have been genuinely attracted to her, at one point begging Winthrop to "acquit [him] of [his] Rudeness if [he] drew off her Glove." When she asked the reason, he retorted there was a great difference "between handling a dead Goat, and a living Lady."[13] Sewall's diary goes on to record a lengthy rudeness on the Madam's part, in contradistinction to what the citizens thought.

And all the town admired for two full years

His excellent address, his gifts of fruit,

Her gracious ways and delicate white ears,

And held the course of nature absolute.

The last line echoes the idea and diction from "As Plato Said": "There is not a more unbending thing / In nature. It is an order that shall find / You out." In the next stanza,

Madam Winthrop asks Sewall to "suffer a peruke," that is, even outside the courtroom to wear a fashionable head cover. The *Diary* relates that he chose instead to wear a velvet cap.

"Madam," he answered her, "I have a Friend
Furnishes me with hair out of His strength,
And he requires only I attend
Unto His charity and to its length."

In his *Diary*, Sewall says, "As to a Perriwig, My best and greatest Friend, I could not possibly have a greater, began to find me with Hair before I was born, and had continued to do so ever since; and I could not find in my heart to go to another."[14] Sewall's humor about his hair's length and the "naked style" of line five turns on his baldness, a detail which the poem omits. Historically, Madam Winthrop hoped the peruke would disguise Sewall's glabrous pate.

Though Winthrop voiced her request in the first month of the courtship, Hecht changed the chronology for effect.

And all the town was witness to his trust:
On Monday he walked out with the Widow Gibbs,
A pious lady of charm and notable bust,
Whose heart beat tolerably beneath her ribs.

The use of "Widow" makes Mrs. Gibbs appear not so attractive as Madam Winthrop, despite the latter's similar widowhood. The poem portrays the romantic contest as a close one. Like the "godly" Winthrop, Gibbs is a "pious lady." Sewall eventually proposes marriage to the less preferred woman, proving the axiom that the sexual law is "a rigor more demanding than precise," as "Divisions upon a Ground" puts it.

A welcomed change for Sewall must have been that the Widow Gibbs' "heart beat tolerably beneath her ribs," whereas Winthrop seemed intolerant about other matters than Sewall's refusal to wear a peruke. Mrs. Gibbs' "notable bust" may also have been instrumental in the decision.

> On Saturday he wrote proposing marriage,
> And closed, imploring that she be not cruel,
> "Your favorable answer will oblige,
> Madam, your humble servant, Samuel Sewall."

The order of the poems leading up to "Samuel Sewall" seems quite calculated. "Divisions upon a Ground," in argumentative mode, exposes society's priggish masking of sexuality. Division four concludes, "The meekest rise to tumble with the proud"; in "Samuel Sewall," the proudest stoops to tumble with the meek (the Widow Gibbs). Two poems after "Divisions" comes "As Plato Said," talking of love as a mathematically precise law. Then follows "Discourse Concerning Temptation," whose opening lines ("Though learned men have been at some dispute /

Touching the taste and color, nature, name / And properties of the Original Fruit")
are intriguing because one such learned man was Samuel Sewall, who wrote a
master's thesis on the nature of original sin. "Samuel Sewall" is thus perfectly "set
up," showing again the careful rhetorical design of *A Summoning of Stones*.

A Baroque Sensibility

Extravagance is Anthony Hecht's favorite poetic pose. This pose, born of his
perception of the world's resplendent excess, manifests itself in exotic words and
affected high diction, sinuous syntax, apparently chaotic but in fact highly controlled grammatical structures, elaborate and quirky rhyme patterns, a curious
wedding of the concrete and abstract, multiple appositives since one will not do,
and an unapologetic fishing for the right word or phrase—all of this a circumlocu-
tive exploration of a subject in order to get at the heart of the matter.[15]

Appropriately, the first of Hecht's poems offered for the world's inspection
in book form, "Double Sonnet," is a paragon of his baroque style. At its core is
the praise of *sprezzatura*, "a grace won by the way from all / Striving in what is
difficult. . . ." Haunting the periphery of the celebration is "the unbidden terror and
bone hand / Of gracelessness, and the unspoken omen / That yet shall render all, by
its first usage, / Speechless, inept, and totally unmanned."

The "sheer extravagance" of the poem's subject calls for double praise, a
"Double Sonnet," for, the hyperbolic persona implies, a single sonnet cannot
contain the effusions called forth by his mystical perception of the world's beauty
concentrated in the movements of a lovely woman. The rhyme scheme (*abba/abba/*
abba/abba // cde/cde/edc/edc), long sentences (each stanza comprises one sentence),

phrases the mind strains to comprehend ("motion made visible," "inflected silence"), and Hecht's repeated use of "all" for its expansive quality contribute to the prestidigitation that evokes in the reader a similar response to the world's pervasive beauty, painfully intensified by the "presage" of beauty's inevitable decay.

"Double Sonnet," by accident or design, takes advantage of Poe's designation of Death as the most melancholy topic and Beauty as the most poetical: "The death, then, of a beautiful woman, is, unquestionably, the most poetical topic in the world—and equally is it beyond doubt that the lips best suited for such topic are those of a bereaved lover." Hecht's poem leaves room for debating whether the persona experiences the woman's loss through death or romantic dissolution, though the second line favors the former interpretation.

> I recall everything, but more than all,
> *Words being nothing now*, an ease that ever
> Remembers her to my unfailing fever. . . .
>   (italics added)

While standing on their own merit, the next lines, to the end of stanza one, recall other poems about love's enrapturing qualities, notably Sir Thomas Wyatt's "They Flee from Me," Herrick's "Upon Julia's Clothes," with its "glittering that taketh me," Frost's "The Silken Tent," also about a woman's lithe poise, and Roethke's "I Knew a Woman," whose subject's lovely bones "moved in circles, and those circles moved."

How she came forward to me, letting fall

Lamplight upon her dress till every small

Motion made visible seemed no mere endeavor

Of body to articulate its offer,

But more a grace won by the way from all

Striving in what is difficult, from all

Losses, so that she moved but to discover

A practice of the blood . . .

. . . .

       . . . as the light fell to favor

Her coming forth; this chiefly I recall.

She moved, that is, in order to kindle his passions for her.

    The "it" that opens stanza two refers to the "grace" of stanza one, a grace that gives its possessor the confidence to win a man to her side without speaking a word. The remainder of the poem captures that first mute but unmistakable gesture of assent by which a woman indicates to a man that his desire for her is matched by hers for him.

It is a part of pride, guiding the hand

At the piano in the splash and passage

Of sacred dolphins, making numbers human

By sheer extravagance . . .

. . . .

Taking no thought at all that man and woman,

Lost in the trance of lamplight, felt the presage

Of the unbidden terror and bone hand

Of gracelessness, and the unspoken omen

That yet shall render all, by its first usage,

Speechless, inept, and totally unmanned.

The "unspoken omen" is the fact, unmentionable at a moment of transport, of mortality. Death's profanation of beauty and love is also given voice in "The Vow," from *The Hard Hours*, by a miscarried fetus who commands its mother, "'turn to my father's lips / Against the time / When his cold hand puts forth its fingertips / Of jointed lime.'" The incantatory style of both poems casts a spell against the Leveler who renders all lovers sexless.

Another sonnet, "Imitation," likewise pays homage to beauty and the immortalizing power of words in the face of beauty's destroyer. The poem's unequivocal statement about the ineffability of love ("Wanting her clear perfection, how may tongues / Manifest what no language understands?") does not prevent the persona from attempting to vocalize its effects on him.

Hecht's use of "all" and of a prolonged sentence in stanza one again achieves the drunkenness caused by the woman's beauty: "Let men take note of her" "And think [that] all glittering enterprise" (worldly success) would be deficient if it lacked "the wide approval of her mouth" (her smile), "And to betoken every man his drouth" (his unquenchable desire for her beauty), we are encouraged to "Drink, in her name, all tankards to their dryness." The poem concludes,

> Yet as her beauty evermore commands
> Even the tanager with tiny lungs
> To flush all silence, may she by these songs
> Know it was love I looked for at her hands.

Though the persona is incapable and unworthy of expressing his love for her or of capturing her beauty, the trope of the last lines indicates that the regal authority of the woman's beauty, like Eve's in Frost's "Never Again Would Birds' Song Be the Same," *forces* him into song.

The showpieces of *A Summoning of Stones*, the two garden poems, exemplify the book's major technique of using objects to launch philosophical meditations.[16] Both are *objets d'arts*, their mirrored rhymes (*abccba* and *abcddcba*) reflecting their subject matter—the paradisal mimes of the Brooklyn botanical gardens and the gardens of the Villa d'Este. Both symbolize "man's brief and natural estate," as "Discourse Concerning Temptation" says, a place "neither Paradise nor Hell, / But of their divers attributes a blend."[17]

"La Condition Botanique," especially its first three stanzas, reveals that man's attempts at human Edens fair not so well as his botanical Edens.[18] The Romans of the first stanza typify the tendency toward debility of post-lapsarian man, indeed of all creation.

Romans, rheumatic, gouty, came

To bathe in Ischian springs where water steamed,

Puffed and enlarged their bold imperial thoughts, and which

Later Madame Curie declared to be so rich

In radioactive content as she deemed

Should win them everlasting fame.

As the arthritic symptoms of rheumatism and gout indicate, an entropic running down of nature occurs outside the paradisal gates. Mankind's trials at reversing the process often backfire, as witness the radioactive Ischian springs and Curie's own death by leukemia. Stanza three introduces the "botanical gardens" of Brooklyn, so solicitous of its plants' comfort that they are elevated to higher life-form status: "each leafy pet [is], / Manured," as a pet may be humanized with manicures, and each, "addressed in Latin," is given royal status thereby. A regulated environment fosters their "thermostatic happiness." Curious world that cares more for its vegetable than its human denizens, that shows "excessive love for the non-human faces," as Auden's poem "A Letter to Lord Byron" puts it. One might imagine Brooklyn as the charter home of Auden's imaginary S.P.C.P.

It won't be long before we find there is

A Society of Everybody's Aunts

For the Prevention of Cruelty to Plants.

Hecht quotes the entire poem in his essay "On W. H. Auden's 'In Praise of Limestone.'"[19]

In the Brooklyn hothouse, the "pipes, like Satan masquerading as the snake, / Coil and uncoil their frightful liquid length," giving the viewers a parabolic vignette of their lost birthright: "And we, like disinherited heirs, / Old Adams, can inspect the void estate / At visiting hours." Eve enters the poem as "Lilith our lady, patroness of plants, / Who sings *Lullay myn lykyng, myn owyn dere derlyng*, / Madrigals nightly to the spiny stalk. . . ." In Jewish mythology, Lilith was often regarded as Adam's first wife. "Lullaby" is a corruption of *Lilla abi* ("Lilith, avaunt"). The literal meaning of "Lilith," "belonging to the night," seems to explain why in Hecht's poem she is depicted as a caretaker who "nightly" sings lullabies to her darling plants. Hecht ignores her more unseemly aspects; after being supplanted by Eve, she becomes a child-molesting night hag. She appears in the Walpurgisnacht scene of Goethe's *Faust* and in Dante Gabriel Rossetti's painting *Lady Lilith*. Rossetti's poem "Body's Beauty," originally titled "Lilith" and written to accompany the painting, claims, "The rose and poppy are her flowers." Perhaps because of this source Hecht calls her "patroness of plants."

Though several critics have noted the virtues of this artificial Eden, I am suspicious that anyone humanly human would care for the relentless regularity of "the lot first given Man, / Sans interruption, as when Universal Pan / Led on the Eternal Spring." This Eternal Spring recalls Stevens' questions, "Is there no change of death in paradise? / Does ripe fruit never fall?" Only in a world where "Death is the mother of beauty" can we know, Stevens argues, "the *heavenly* fellowship / Of men that perish."

The double simile of the pipes, "like Satan masquerading as the snake," reminds us that Eden was no less deceptive than Brooklyn's mimetic paradise where weak plants put on a show of fearsomeness. "The spears of chive" help "The sensitive plant" feign "its dread," as does

> The Mexican flytrap, that can knit
> Its quilled jaws pitilessly, and would hurt
> A fly with pleasure. . . .

This is predatory nature, "red in tooth and claw," not really "the unconditional garden spot, / [Its] effortless innocence preserved" of stanza eight. Just as the world's original citizens were evicted from their Garden by the eastern gate, Brooklyn's citizens "think, as [they] depart by the toll gate: / No one has lived here these five thousand years." This air of lamentation should not prevent our asking, "Would anyone *want* to live there?" Such stasis, epitomized in stanza six's "leading Riley's life in bed," though perhaps initially attractive to those whose body tends to weakness and immobility, would doubtless grow tedious after a few thousand years. Presented with these antipodal worlds, many uninsane people would choose "the world . . . all before them" of Milton's evicted tenants over the sameness everywhere of traditional Eden.

The movement of "La Condition Botanique" is dialectical, as if its persona cannot make up his mind about the world that is "neither Paradise nor Hell, / But of their divers attributes a blend." The spinning flux of stanza nine captures the dizzy busy-ness of "man's brief and natural estate."

Our world is turned on points, is whirled

On wheels, Tibetan prayer wheels, French verb wheels,

The toothy wheels of progress, the terrible torque

Insisting, and in the sky even above New York

Rotate the marvelous four-fangled seals

Ezekiel saw. . . .

There is something "marvelous" about this vertiginous motion, though, as with stasis, one would not want to endure it for eternity. Seeming to want both worlds forever, the persona can have neither. Death is a disadvantage of our world, but "Death is the mother of beauty," as Stevens says and Hecht's tenth stanza affirms. "The mother-of-pearled"

Home of the bachelor oyster lies

Fondled in fluent shifts of bile and lime

As sunlight strikes the water, and it is of our world,

And will appear to us sometime where the finger is curled

Between the frets upon a mandolin,

Fancy cigar boxes, and eyes

Of ceremonial masks; and all

The places where Kilroy inscribed his name,

. . . .

> And all these various things are of our world.
>
> But what's become of Paradise?

Even the death of an oyster may enhance the beauty of mandolins, ceremonial masks, or mundane cigar boxes. With an oyster shell as handy magic marker, Kilroy, the representative and ubiquitous American soldier, can write his name and add comic relief to a painful world while simultaneously betraying the genesis of many wars, territoriality. In the poem's paradise, Kilroy is the modern Adam who labels his possessions like a dog saluting each passing hydrant.

Polyphemus, Buddha, Kilroy, and a Civil War veteran in stanzas eleven and twelve indicate that war knows no temporal, religious, or topographical boundaries. Stanza thirteen discovers the persona wanting back his rejected paradise. The visitors "stare through the glass panes," the veil separating them from the symbolic paradise, but ultimately turn away

> . . . to strengthen our poor breath
> And body, keep the flesh rosy with hopeful dreams,
> Peach-colored, practical, to decorate the bones, with schemes
> Of life insurance, Ice-Cream-After-Death,
> Hormone injections, against the *mort'*
>
> *Saison*, largely to babble praise
> Of Simeon Pyrites, patron saint

> Of our Fools' Paradise, whose glittering effigy
>
> Shines in God's normal sunlight till blind men see
>
> Visions as permanent as artists paint. . . .

It is a Fools' Paradise where people hope for eternal life and eternal youth. Even as people attempt suspended animation via hormone injections and life insurance, they know the foolishness of the gesture. In Simeon Pyrites, Hecht telescopes holy men of three dispensations into one fabricated saint whose last name, a neat alteration of Simeon Stylites, is synonymous with fool's gold. The Simeon of Genesis 29.33 heads one of Israel's twelve tribes. The Simeon of Luke 2 was promised "that he should not see death, before he had seen the Lord's Christ." Simeon Stylites, a Syrian Christian ascetic, lived and preached atop a sixty-foot pillar for thirty years. Each of these Simeons held claim to a promise of immortality, though none was foolish enough to believe in the permanence of this world that the Brooklynites long for.

The futility of these feeble attempts at stasis creates a yearning for the immortality of art, of Keats' painted urn where the lovers are transfixed in the perfectly ecstatic moment of anticipation, both Being and Becoming put on eternal hold. The final stanza shows the persona's resignation, a retraction of his rebellious attitude in the poem. Like Milton's Adam, he eventually accepts his ambiguous "punishment."

> In open field or public bed
>
> With ultraviolet help, man hopes to learn

The leafy secret, pay his most outstanding debt
To God in the salt and honesty of his sweat,
And in his streaming face manly to earn
His daily and all-nourishing bread.

Here is embodied the theologically traditional idea of the ennobling quality of work, a tenet of both Romanticism and Puritanism. Though Brooklyn's greenhouse elicits longings for a workless paradise, the botanical condition of the title is not an attractive alternative. The gardens are, after all, an imitation paradise made by man of fallen substance whose fate is as predictable as that of the "old South Boston Aquarium" which, in Lowell's poem, "stands / in a Sahara of snow now," broken windows boarded. One can easily imagine a time when Brooklyn's conservatory, "Where green lies ageless under snow-stacked roofs," is similarly in ruin.

Hecht's poem and garden may better be interpreted not merely as nostalgically Edenic but also as hopefully Utopian, anticipatory of a time when man's technology gives him a reprieve from the Old Testament curse of stanza fifteen ("In the sweat of thy face shalt thou manage, said the Lord"), as it already in large part has, thus freeing him to engage in leisurely activities such as writing poems about a new paradise.

There is something wholesome about the poem's last line, where man earns his daily bread with salty honesty, yet its rhetoric also reminds that man does not live by bread alone, but by "the fleshed Word" of stanza fifteen. Given this injunction, man can still lead a joyous life of discovery, hoping "to learn / the leafy secret"—

how, through photosynthesis, plants gather substance from sunlight. Man thus hopes to learn effortless self-sufficiency, how to get food without sweating. The vision is optimistic, the poem manifesting the metamorphosis of man from scratching the earth with bent back and bowed head to an unindentured *homo erectus* on the verge of dominating nature and, having paid "his outstanding debt / To God," preparing to pace off the boundaries of his new paradise, if not yet break the ground. In *The Machine in the Garden*, Leo Marx talks about the modern machine encroaching on, tainting, or replacing the Edenic garden. Brooklyn's botanical gardens, as Hecht sees them, have put the machine to creating oases where their flourishing was formerly impossible.

Of the showpieces, "The Gardens of the Villa d'Este," more wholeheartedly and lightheartedly celebratory of man's "brief and natural estate," is arguably the superior poem because, like the fountains it describes, it moves smoothly and directly to its close whereas "La Condition Botanique," with its dandling imagery and darting scene changes, has no such happy wedding of form and content.

"The Gardens" takes as premise the conclusion of "Botanique," that the current world is preferable to unchanging paradise. The formal gardens, stanza ten flatly states, are an aphrodisiacal microcosm of the-world-as-it-is: "Actually, it is real / The way the world is real," and "a style can teach us how / To know the world in little. . . ." No antiseptic paradise, the garden makes room for "The wood louse, the night crawler, the homespun / Spider" and the "green invasion" of moss.

The blatant and subtle sexuality of the poem's language gives the feel of the world's pervasive, yeasty fermentation, the "urge and urge and urge" of Whitman's procreant world—the "opposite equals" in Hecht's poem, no less than in Whitman's, seeking to be knitted, as evidenced in the double meaning of "The sum / Of intersecting [plant or human] limbs was something planned." The antithesis of Marvell's garden, which proclaims, "Two paradises 'twere in one / To live in Paradise alone," Hecht's welcomes the itch of sex and scratches it at every opportunity. The mating pairs from mythology, history, nature, and the persona's life bear this out: Hephaestus and Aphrodite, Adonis and Venus, Figaro and Suzanne, "Pliny's pregnant mouse, bearing unborn within her / Lewd sons and pregnant daughters," the persona and Susan.

In stanza one's phrase, the poem portrays a paradise "not beyond our reach." The second stanza's invocation of the muse indicates the epic nature of the poem and garden in which, we gather as the poem rolls along, every sexual participant is a hero.

> Goddess, be with me now;
> Commend my music to the woods.
> There is no garden to the practiced gaze
> Half so erotic: here the sixteenth century thew
> Rose to its last perfection, this being chiefly due
> To the provocative role the water plays.
> Tumble and jump, the fountains' moods
> Teach the world how.

The "provocative role" of water, throughout the poem associated with the feminine principle, gives "rise" to a "thew," ordinarily meaning a well-developed muscle, but here taking on phallic connotations. (The word's cognates are revelatory: thumb, tumescent, tumor, tuber.) The fountains "teach the world how" to "tumble and jump" in "the bed / Of jonquils" or "the linen bed" of stanza one. The heretofore discussed law of sex appears in the last half of stanza three.

> Ligorio, the laurel! Every turn and quirk
> Weaves in this waving green and liquid world to work
> Its formula, binding upon the gland,
> Even as molecules succumb
> To Avogadro's law.

Just as Avogadro's law indicates the uniformity of the sexual law, the water's "Brownian movement" in stanza six argues the randomness of its expression or choice of partners. The principle in action is seen in stanza nine: "It was in such a place / That Mozart's Figaro contrived / The totally expected." The commended "Ligorio" above is Pirro Ligorio, "one of the chief artistic creators of the Villa," "designer of the Villa d'Este gardens," "one of the leading archaeologists" of the sixteenth century, and the "private archaeologist" of the Cardinal of Ferrara (Ippolito II d'Este, 1509-1572), a great patron of the arts.[20]

The mythic and mystic aspects of sex are suggested in the metaphor of stanza four. The "mesh of trees" plots to "capture alive" the "tourist soul" with the "artifice of an Hephaestus' net." More erotica in stanza five, where "flesh" represents male, "water" female, and "inclines" an erection: "The whole garden inclines / The flesh

as water falls, to seek / For depth." Stanza seven is more obvious: "White /
Ejaculations leap to teach / How fertile are these nozzles."

Spurted from the breasts of harpies, the water fills flumes, leaps ledges, and
stops in a pool where it, "by a plumber's ruse, / Rises again to laugh and squirt / At
heaven." This "plumber's ruse" may be Ligorio's "hydraulic device of the Fountain
of the Owl adopted from Hero of Alexandria's writings," a treatise on hydraulics
that refers to "'automatic machines which are moved by the striking of
wheels. . . .'"[21] Like the engines of sex, the garden is a perpetual motion machine,
never seeming to run out of energy, constantly renewing itself. The persona traces
this cycle again, the streams finally passing "To lily-padded ease, where insubor-
dinate lass / And lad can cool their better parts, where sun / Heats them again to
furnace pitch / To prove his law is light." Later, the persona argues more thoroughly
that the chaotic element constantly strives to break out of constricting form, as here
the insubordination of lass and lad implies rebellion against the social order represented in the garden's formality. The sun proves "his law is light" in that its gravity
helps the streams ("by a plumber's ruse") to defy gravity. The social application is
that courting rituals (society's laws) provide rules for the predictable and usually
flexible (thereby the law is "light") expression of love.

The poem moves from general statements about order and sex to more and more
demonstratively particular examples. In stanza eleven, the readers, "honorable
guests," are allowed first to be auditeurs, then voyeurs,

                    Hearing in the velure of darkness impish strings
                    Mincing Tartini, hearing the hidden whisperings:

> *"Carissima*, the moon gives too much light,"
>> Though by its shining it invests
>>> Her bodice with such gains

>> As show their shadowed worth
>> Deep in the cleavage. . . .

The lovers "give way to their delight" in abandon "While overhead the stars resolve / Every extravagance." The freedom, the sexual license, of the couple seems to be lost (dissolved) in and perhaps even forgiven (absolved) by the universe's great, orderly design, as depicted in the grandeur of the heavenly constellations where heroes are on allegorical display. The huge motions of the zodiac follow a perfect and inexorable order that seems not to notice or care about earthly extravaganzas or breaches of conduct.

After the night's debauchery, "Gardeners will come to resurrect / Downtrodden iris" and generally restore order, but will impishly "pass / Over the liberal effect" of moss growing "upon the statue's shoulder." The moss, called "Caprice and cunning spawn" because it seems to spread randomly (with the conspiratorial connivance of the gardeners), embodies Herrick's notion of "Delight in Disorder," as indeed does the whole poem.

>> For thus it was designed:
>> Controlled disorder at the heart

> Of everything, the paradox, the old
> Oxymoronic itch to set the formal strictures
> Within a natural context, where the tension lectures
> Us on our mortal state, and by controlled
> Disorder, labors to keep art
> From being too refined.

Compare the stanza's last couplet to that of Herrick's poem: "A sweet disorder in [various articles of women's clothing] / Do more bewitch me, than when art / Is too precise in every part." Hecht's stanza is not only about the gardens of the Villa d'Este. It is a little dissertation on the world, with punning commentary on the New Critical principles of structure, texture, and the distorting tensions between meaning and meter, as well as between the barren abstractions of science and the rich "local textures" of the objects of poetry.[22] The moss in the garden would be analogous to a poem's non-necessary texture, whose excess works against the poem's "logical argument" in the same manner that the moss works against the garden's formality. In "The Gardens of the Villa d'Este," pure form and chaotic substance do allegorical battle for Hecht.

The poem's argument is cousin, too, to Frost's notion of "how a poem can have wildness and at the same time a subject that shall be fulfilled."[23] The smooth forward motion of the garden's water and Hecht's poem, in fact, is suspiciously like the rhetoric of Frost's famous formulation of "the figure a poem makes":

> It begins in delight, it inclines to the impulse, it assumes direction with the first line laid down, it runs a course of lucky events, and ends in a clarification of life—not necessarily a great clarification such as sects and cults are founded on, but in a momentary stay against confusion.[24]

Though I have gone to some pains to discuss the meaning of the garden poems, the poems are certainly also about themselves. Forcing unmanageable plants or words into shapes or meter, a gardener or poet finds stubble that will not behave. The form of the gardens shows "where by dint of force / D'Estes have set their seal." Just as obvious is the dint of Hecht's force on his stanzas, which give the impression of being stamped from a seal. And, just as "the garden must allow / For the recalcitrant," so with the stuff of poetry, as the shapes of Hecht's stanzaic topiary betray. Each stanza has mirrored rhyme (*abcddcba*), regular accentual-syllabic meter (6-8-10-12-12-10-8-6), and pleasingly beveled left edges. But the intractable, stickly stuff of language makes for a ragged right edge. "The garden [and poetry] must allow / For the recalcitrant; a style can teach us how / To know the world in little where the weed / Has license. . . ."

Among the several casts the poem conforms to, it fits most snugly the *carpe diem* stamp, notably the "Come live with me and be my love" series of Marlowe, Ralegh, Donne, and C. Day Lewis. Having, the reader assumes, duly impressed his girl with the beauty of the verses he has written her, the persona comes to the point.

> Susan, it had been once
>
> My hope to see this place with you,
>
> See it as in the hour of thoughtless youth.
>
> For age mocks all diversity, its genesis,
>
> And whispers to the heart, *"Cor mio*, beyond all this
>
> Lies the unchangeable and abstract truth,"
>
> Claims of the grass, it is not true,
>
> And makes our youth its dunce.

The uses of "valentines" in stanza five and of "heart" in both English and Italian make the poem typically romantic. The last two stanzas, in their insistence on a love higher than base sexual attraction, differentiate it from that tradition. No longer a thoughtless youth (compare Wordsworth's "Tintern Abbey": "For I have learned / To look on nature, not as in the hour / Of thoughtless youth"), the persona wishes not to be thought of as age's dunce, either. Age, possessing memory but not desire, "mocks" or derides diversity, the genesis of its metamorphosis,[25] claiming that grass, like flesh, "is not true," does not endure and is not faithful. There seems a transference of infidelity from lovers to the grass whereon they took their pleasure. At another time, the lovers may lie on the same plot of grass with others, thus making youth the dunce of age, since youth's naive promises of eternal fidelity are repeatedly broken. Also, age makes a dunce of youth if youth does not take advantage at every opportunity of things accessible only during youth.

The persona realizes that the attitude of the aged is more "sour grapes" than spriritual wisdom, and, in the last stanza, succumbs to the forces of physical and spiritual love just as the garden's foliage weaves in its "liquid world to work / Its formula, binding upon the gland, / Even as molecules succumb / To Avogadro's law." The mock-logical conclusion of "To His Coy Mistress" ("Now therefore / . . . let us sport us while we may") seems consciously adopted in Hecht's ultimate stanza.

> Therefore, some later day
> Recall these words, let them be read
> Between us, let them signify that here
> Are more than formulas, that age sees no more clearly
> For its poor eyesight, and philosophy grows surly,
> That falling water and the blood's career
> Lead down the garden path to bed
> And win us both to May.

If "here are more than formulas," more than mere lusty attraction, Susan stands to gain more than a momentary pleasure on the "garden path." Wordsworth, too, after "the hour of thoughtless youth" saw more in nature than "present pleasure": "life and food / For future years" and "A presence that disturbs me with the joy / of elevated thoughts." Or maybe after all, this is just another one of those ruses in the poet-lover's repertoire of flatteries and subterfuges, as demonstrated by the address of Marvell's persona in "To His Coy Mistress," Donne's in "The Flea," or a dozen dozen in their place. In fact, the decaying of the penultimate stanza and a-maying of the ultimate stanza align the poem with another famous ploy, found in Herrick's "Corinna's Going A-Maying," the concluding rhymes of which drive home the choice: "Then, while time serves, and we are but decaying, / Come, my Corinna, come, let's go a-Maying." Despite the derisive sermonizing of the aged, given the choice between decaying and a-maying, Hecht's persona is no dunce. Though the poem seems to have gotten away, in its last two stanzas, from the gardens of the Villa d'Este (its ostensible subject), the "falling water" and "blood's career" remind us of the association of femininity and masculinity with water and (rising) "blood." A disingenuous rereading of "The Gardens of the Villa d'Este" reveals that the poem, from stanza one, drives to its conclusion with Susan in mind all along as recipient of the epistle.

As a footnote to this discussion of "The Gardens of the Villa d'Este," I point out its similarities to Richard Wilbur's "A Baroque Wall-Fountain in the Villa Sciarra." Both poems came of their authors' stay in Italy as Prix de Rome fellows, Hecht in 1951, Wilbur in 1954. What Wilbur has said about his poem applies equally to Hecht's: "Of course, a lot of the length in this poem—a lot of the length of sentence—has to do with an effort to imitate the trickling down of the water," Hecht's mimetic syntax faring better in its duty because it is more convoluted. The theme of both poems is likewise similar. Again, Wilbur, abbreviated: "It's a descriptive poem about this and other fountains, but my subject is pleasure and what place it has in life."[26]

The War Poems

The points of truisms are often dulled by their frequent contact with thick skulls.

However platitudinous it sounds, in this world it is "almost impossible not to hurt anyone / Whether by action or inaction," as "A Voice at a Seance," from *Shadows*, says. Hecht possesses a profound sense of this "sad knowledge." What bothers him no less is that peace and progress seem inextricably linked to war and exploitation. Focusing on these themes, "A Roman Holiday" is a jeremiad that voices Hecht's feelings and frustrations in a most general way, sweeping across history for examples of achievement at the expense of fratricide. As might be expected, since he clings to topics that move him,[27] exploring their nuances in recyclings, Hecht does not abandon the theme of the world's indigenous pain in his later work but instead, as in *Shadows*, gives it immediacy in "The Cost," where a young Italian couple is oblivious that their freedom was purchased at the great human expense of wars, and intimacy in "Black Boy in the Dark," where the uneducated are exploited for corporate profit.

Much ado has been made of the guilt of war survivors.[28] Than guilt, Hecht's own war poems seem more tinged with a sense of surprise at survival and of responsibility because of that survival, with the added burden of knowing that fulfillment of such responsibility is impossible. In "A Roman Holiday," behind the larger statements about war and the implication of a latent germ of evil at the heart of humanity, lies a sense of personal responsibility for some kind of success and a feeling of guilt at realizing that no success could atone for the crimes committed in the persona's World War, much less all of the world's wars. Lost in the panorama of historical carnage, overwhelmed by the long sentences expressing that carnage, is the short "I write from Rome" of the first and forty-first lines. The line forces the reader to identify the persona as Hecht, writing from Rome during his stay there for winning the 1951 Prix de Rome. The "Roman Holiday" of the title implies "an entertainment which causes loss or suffering to those providing it," so called from the "gladiatorial contests staged as entertainment for the ancient Romans." The term derives from Byron's reference in *Childe Harold's Pilgrimage* to the gladiators as "butchered to make a Roman holiday."[29] Thus, the persona enjoys a time of peace bought by the War and enjoys a holiday at the financial expense of a grantor.

Coincidentally, Richard Wilbur's Roman holiday for the 1954 Prix de Rome produced "A Baroque Wall-Fountain in the Villa Sciarra," also written under the impetus of guilt: "I had a fellowship and felt obliged to turn out some work as well as enjoy myself." The linking of obligation with enjoyment neatly matches Hecht's sense of responsibility brought on by war survival and to a lesser degree by the Prix de Rome and Guggenheims in 1954 and 1959, which produced, further down the line, the humorous "Application for a Grant":

> Noble executors of the munificent testament
> Of the late John Simon Guggenheim, distinguished bunch
> Of benefactors, there are certain kinds of men
> Who set their hearts on being bar tenders,
>
> . . . .
>
> One man may have a sharp nose for tax shelters,
> Screwing the IRS with mirth and profit;
>
> . . . .
>
> As for me, the prize for poets . . .
>
> . . . .

Would supply my modest wants, who dream of nothing

But a pad on Eighth Street and your approbation.

After this digression, we return to the study of war. The movement of "A Roman Holiday" is inductive. It catalogs particular instances of mutual hatred and destruction, concluding with the general view that revenge, by definition, perpetuates itself *ad infinitum.*

The poem, built of strata-like stanzas, concerns what may be termed the archaeology of blood. Its prolonged grammatical structure imparts the layering effect of history. In stanza one, the "pilgrims came to see" the Colosseum. In stanza two, the reader having to remember and supply the elided subject "pilgrims," they "came to see where Caesar Augustus turned / Brick into marble. . . ." In stanza three, the again unmentioned pilgrims "see the wealthy, terraced Palatine. . . ." In this stanza, the elided subject is dropped and replaced by a "daydreaming employee" who "has forgotten" and, at the beginning of stanza four, "has forgot" certain historical facts. Similarly, stanza five begins, "there was wisdom even then that said" several things: "Nothing endures" (line 2), "Sands shift in the wind, petals are shed" (line 3), and "Eternal cities also are undone" (line 4). Line 5 of stanza five begins with "Informed," forcing the reader to make the difficult grammatical transition, made more complicated by the capital letter and previous semicolon, both of which lead the reader, initially, to treat line five as a new grammatical and semantic unit. Also, the repetition of "that," which would ordinarily signal grammatical parallelism in lines two through four, has been foregone. The link of lines one and five is the subject "wisdom" that "said" the things in lines two through

four and "[that] Informed," in line five, "the living and the pious dead / That there
is no new thing under the sun." Here is the full stanza:

> Yet there was wisdom even then that said,
>
> Nothing endures at last but only One;
>
> Sands shift in the wind, petals are shed,
>
> Eternal cities also are undone;
>
> Informed the living and the pious dead
>
> That there is no new thing under the sun,
>
> Nor can the best ambition come to good
>
> When it is founded on a brother's blood.

What is achieved by this technique is the feeling of geological layering, as in the
poem cities are built on the layered foundations of brother-blood.

Stanza one is a mini-history of the Colosseum from its dedication by Titus in
A.D. 81 with a hundred days of gladiatorial combats, to its consecration by Pope
Benedict XIV (r. 1740-1758) to the Passion of Christ, in commemoration of the
martyrs' blood shed there. Thus, it is "pagan ground, turned to our good":

> I write from Rome. Last year, the Holy Year,
>
> The flock was belled, and pilgrims came to see
>
> How milkweed mocked the buried engineer,
>
> Wedging between his marble works, where free

And famished went the lions forth to tear

A living meal from the offending knee,

And where, on pagan ground, turned to our good,

Santa Maria sopra Minerva stood.

The history lesson continues in the second stanza, whose grammatical subject is "pilgrims," from the poem's second line:

And came to see where Caesar Augustus turned

Brick into marble, thus to celebrate

Apollo's Peace, that lately had been learned,

And where the Rock that bears the Church's weight,

Crucified Peter, raised his eyes and yearned

For final sight of heavenly estate,

But saw ungainly huge above his head

Our stony base to which the flesh is wed.

After familial and civil struggles and long, scattered, severe wars, Augustus achieved a peace (a Roman holiday) during which he improved the people, corrected governmental abuses, suppressed luxury, reformed the military, instituted public police and fire departments, and reorganized the monetary system. Indeed, as the famous line that Hecht alters claims, "He found it of brick and left it of marble."

The pilgrims also came to see "the Rock," "Crucified Peter" (the martyr's tomb is under the main altar of St. Peter's Basilica), who, when he "raised his eyes" for a final glimpse of the heavens, saw above him "our stony base to which the flesh is wed," that is, the ground, because he was crucified upside-down. Our flesh is wed to the earth because we are made of it, as Adam (whose name means "earth") was, and because we tend to be, according to the moralistic man, inordinately attached to the world.

Stanza three introduces a guard who serves as Hecht's ironic representative of the forgetful beneficiaries (*i.e.*, most people) of past wars.

> And see the wealthy, terraced Palatine,
> Where once the unknown god or goddess ruled
> In mystery and silence, whose divine
> Name has been lost or hidden from the fooled,
> Daydreaming employee who guards the shrine
> And has forgotten how men have been schooled
> To hide the Hebrew Vowels, that craft or sin
> Might not pronounce their sacred origin.

The continual supplanting of people and beliefs is captured in the Hebrew God's usurpation of the unknown Roman god or goddess. The hidden "Hebrew Vowels" refer to the Tetragrammaton, also alluded to in "A Poem for Julia." And not only has our symbolic "guard" of history forgotten the Judeo-Christian heritage of the spot he watches over, but he has also forgotten his native mythology.

> And has forgot that on the temple floor
> Once was a Vestal Virgin overcome
> Even by muscle of the god of war,
> And ran full of unearthly passion home,
> Being made divinity's elected whore
> And fertile with the twins that founded Rome.
> Columns are down. Unknown the ruined face
> Of travertine, found in a swampy place.

Fraternal rivalries, the poem's theme, are an integral part of Rome's founding. Numitor, early king and one of Aeneas' men, is dethroned by his brother Amulius, who made Rhea Silvia, Numitor's daughter, a vestal virgin. Not by accident does the myth have Mars, god of war, ravish Rhea, who gives birth to Romulus and Remus. Murder begets murder, as Hecht is at pains to point out. Rhea is killed, the twins thrown into the Tiber. Washed ashore, they are suckled by a she-wolf and raised by a herdsman and wife. Eventually, they overthrow Amulius, restore Numitor, and set out to build a city. In an argument over its location, Romulus kills Remus, and the rest, as they say, is history.

An earmark of much of Hecht's moral verse is an occasional, seemingly irresistible, hit-and-run Ecclesiastical pronouncement about the ultimate decay of this world's vanities, as in the Ozymandias-like reference to "the ruined face / Of travertine" above and the shifting sands below:

> Yet there was wisdom even then that said,
> Nothing endures at last but only One;
> Sands shift in the wind, petals are shed,
> Eternal cities also are undone;
> Informed the living and the pious dead
> That there is no new thing under the sun,
> Nor can the best ambition come to good
> When it is founded on a brother's blood.

The specific examples of hatred and homicide coalesce here in a generalized thematic statement. The founding of kingdoms and their subsequent histories seem fraught with fratricide or kin hatred: Cain and Abel, Romulus and Remus, Jacob and Esau, Joseph and his brothers. The next stanza brings us back to the present and the poem's burden on the persona.

> I write from Rome. It is late afternoon
> Nearing the Christmas season. Blooded light
> Floods through the Colosseum, where platoon
> And phalanx of the Lord slaved for the might

Of Titus' pleasure. Blood repeats its tune
Loudly against my eardrums as I write,
And recollects what they were made to pay
Who out of worship put their swords away.

Against the backdrop of this particular poem, it should be remembered that the root of "gladiator" is the Latin *gladius*, sword. The persona's pulse fluttering his eardrums is personified as the blood of the Christian martyrs whispering reminders of his debt to them. Their putting their swords away recalls Isaiah 2.4, "And he shall judge among the nations, and shall rebuke many people: and they shall beat their swords into plowshares, and their spears into pruninghooks: nation shall not lift up sword against nation, neither shall they learn war any more." Here and elsewhere in his poetry, Hecht invokes the Christian ethic as a harmonizing solution to an otherwise endless cycle of vengeance and re-vengeance. The final stanza, however, sees no end to humankind's civil war.

The bells declare it. "Crime is at the base,"
Rings in the belfry where the blood is choired.
Crime stares from the unknown, ruined face,
And the cold wind, endless and wrath-inspired,
Cries out for judgment in a swampy place
As darkness claims the trees. "Blood is required,
And it shall fall," below the Seven Hills
The blood of Remus whispers out of wells.

The dismal attitude of the poem's conclusion persists through *The Hard Hours*, where more personal and painful examples of war's carnage are put on cathartic display and perhaps exorcised, so that it is a relief to read the more optimistic poems gathered in *Millions of Strange Shadows*.

From the general commentary on the nature and causes of war that "A Roman Holiday" is, I turn to "Christmas Is Coming," an allegorical treatment of war and pain that takes the raw images confronting an infantry soldier's vision and translates his experience into the universal struggle for survival. The Christmas setting in the present poem and in "A Roman Holiday" reminds the reader of the unrealized "peace on earth, good will to men" that the Christ child is supposed to bring. Though heat and blood are often associated with war or hatred, in the poem warmth and blood represent compassion and sympathy, now lost.

In the first stanza, the poor "go wandering the hills at night, / Gunning for enemies" among the grass that is "fossilized" by the cold. A segment from an old British nursery rhyme, spoken by an elderly beggar at Christmas, serves as the second stanza:

> *Christmas is coming. The goose is getting fat.*
> *Please put a penny in the Old Man's hat.*

The image of a homeless, starving person begging for food at Christmas, a time of gift-sharing, is pitiful. The next line asks, "Where is the warmth of blood?" Where is compassion?

At the subsistence level, fine distinctions are lost. Any sound becomes generic "sound," important only because it can betray one's position and bring death.

> . . . The enemy
> Has ears than can hear clearly in the cold,
> Can hear the shattering of fossil grass,
> Can hear the stiff cloth rub against itself,
> Making a sound. . . .

Despite pain, the soldier must remain quiet. Words and images called up by "lamb" include the warmth of wool, a holiday feast, domesticity, a paschal lamb, the Lamb of God, and sacrifice in general, but especially, here, *lack* of communion.

> The skin freezes to metal. One must crawl
> Quietly in the dark. Where is the warmth?
> The lamb has yielded up its fleece and warmth
> And woolly life, but who shall taste of it?
> Here on the ground one cannot see the stars.
> The lamb is killed. *The goose is getting fat.*

Face-down to avoid detection, the soldier cannot reckon his position by the stars' guidance, nor does he have time to enjoy their beauty or ponder their religious significance or symbology. By this point, the unshared Christmas goose of the wealthy is surrealistically turning into the menacing goose step of a growing Nazi Germany.

The soldier knows he is getting closer to his enemy by "bits of string" and "pieces of foil" they have left behind. Soon, the soldier will have to sensitize his frozen fingers in order to pull the trigger. He "must find out thistles to remember pain."

> Reach for the brambles, crawl to them and reach,
> Clutching for thorns, search carefully to feel
> The point of thorns, life's crown, *the Old Man's hat.*

The thorns compose life's crown because, by cutting his fingers with them, the soldier can restore the circulation and sensation needed to pull a trigger. Numbness, associated with death, is worse than pain, which, life-giving, is also here death-delivering; the soldier sensitizes his hands in order to kill his enemy. The Old Man's hat merges, dreamlike, with Christ's crown, symbol simultaneously of pain and death, and of redemption and life. The poem closes,

> *If you haven't got a penny, a ha'penny will do,*
> *If you haven't got a ha'penny, God bless you.*

Though it is difficult to pin down any one-to-one correspondences of image and meaning in the poem, its drift seems to be towards recovering lost compassion, an achievement which entails sympathizing and doing unto others as one would be done by.

"Japan," more particular than "A Roman Holiday" or "Christmas Is Coming," deals, not with individuals, but with a race, one of the Axis powers. The poem's rhetoric is based on the deceptiveness of appearances in general, but especially concerns the diminutive size of the Japanese. When the persona was a child, he thought of the "miniature country" as "Home of the Short," an "academy of stunts" (tricks or stunted people) where the race, all circus performers to his limited vision, was trained.

In the present tense of the poem, the persona's country occupies postwar Japan, and the speaker is warned by Intelligence and the War Department against "treachery compounding in their brains / Like mating weasels." Yet he finds the Japanese docile and deferential, their quaint accent while explaining their agricultural system "a shy sign of brotherhood / In the old human bondage to the facts / Of day-to-day existence." Waving their hands to help along their halting expression, they remind him of ants "Signaling tiny pacts / With their antennae. . . ." In light of what siblings do in "A Roman Holiday," brotherly love is suspect. Thus, "Brotherhood" and "bondage" are in appropriate opposition and in concord with the reference to "Cain's own image" in the next stanza.

Stanza six lays out one of the poem's themes: "Human endeavor clumsily betrays / Humanity." In the field of war, Japan's early success at "Pearl and Wake" and later defeat testify to this truth. In the agricultural field, their attempts are as ambiguous. They plant rice in water and, using "excrement" for fertilizer, grow "Schistosomiasis / Japonica, that enters through / The pores into the avenue / And

orbit of the blood, where it may foil / The heart and kill, or settle in the brain." This
example, enlarged, comments on the ambiguity of even the best human intentions.[30]

Now initiated into the brotherhood of deceit, this man puts away childish things.

> Now the quaint early image of Japan
> That was so charming to me as a child
> Seems like a bright design upon a fan,
>
> . . . .
>
> A river which the wrist can stop
> With a neat flip, revealing merely sticks
> And silk of what had been a fan before,
>   And like such winning tricks,
> It shall be buried in excelsior.

The image of the last line is not only of putting childhood's toys in storage, but also
of carefully packing away something quaint and valuable in wood shavings. The
choice of "buried" calls up Hiroshima and Nagasaki, also buried in rubble.
Bolstering this reading is the image of stanza two, "Fragile and easily destroyed,
/ Those little boats of celluloid / Driven by camphor round the bathroom sink," a
microcosmic image which brings to mind the postwar saw of our shrinking world.

"Drinking Song," more particular and personal, brings together the major
countries in the western theater of World War II. The American speaker's platoon
has captured a German headquarters, a palace that holds Italian art and French

cognac. A week before, "The women of this house" "prayed to God" "For mercy, forgiveness, and the death of us." The persona thinks of the prayer as ironically answered.

> We are indeed diminished.
>   We are twelve.
> But have recaptured a sufficiency
> Of France's cognac; and it shall be well,
> Given sufficient time, if we can down
> Half of it, being as we are, reduced.

The soldier repays irony with irony, depicting his platoon as "twelve" disciples of war at a drunken last supper. "Reduced" may echo *Il Duce*, just as "living room," also at the end of a line to call attention to itself, is a literal translation of *Lebensraum*:

> Five dead in the pasture, yet they loom
> As thirstily as ever. Are recalled
> By daring wagers to this living room:
> "I'll be around to leak on your grave."

In his tavern drinking song, the persona toasts a portrait of Beatrice d'Este in the first stanza and, in the last stanza, his rifle, dubbed after Roland's sword, now safely holstered.

> And *Durendal*, my only *Durendal*,
> Thou hast preserved me better than a sword;
> Rest in the enemy umbrella stand
> While that I measure out another drink.
> I am beholden to thee, by this hand,
> This measuring hand. We are beholden all.

The poem's form fits the action of its jolly topers. The rhyme scheme starts off regular, *abcd*, immediately starts breaking down, *bace/dfeg*, slips at mid-poem where the line splits and drops, and lapses into drunken freedom in the final fifteen lines, which contain only three rhymes. The pattern imitates the movement from the regimen of war to the chaos of victory.

The title "A Deep Breath at Dawn" promises to contain either the joy of an aubade or the lamentation of an alba. The deep breath is, instead, a sigh of relief. Having stayed awake throughout the night, not with a lover, but with the "ghost" of a war buddy, the persona is relieved to see the unsuperstitious "rational light" of morning "When, at the birdcall, all the ghosts were gone."

The two succeeding stanzas survey the relationship of Mars and Venus, singling out as sacred to Mars "the wolf, the fig tree, and the woodpecker." Stanza three has characteristics of an aubade, its prepositional phrases giving the effect of a viewer's eye jumping from object to object as it takes in the scenery: "above the scene / Cluttered with dandelions, near the fence," and so on. The stanza is announced, however, by the statement, "Morning deceived him those six years ago." Because of the landscape's beauty and serenity, "the war / Seemed elsewhere." Stanza five's last couplet interrupts the reverie with the shock of a bullet's impact: "And he could feel in his body, driven home, / The wild tooth of the wolf that suckled Rome." The teats of the wolf that suckled Romulus and Remus are often said to be metaphorical representations of the city's seven hills. The "wild tooth," then, would be a bullet made of metal mined from the Italian earth (mother). Stanzas four and five are similar to the concluding irony of *All Quiet on the Western Front* when the soldier's death comes in the silence of a war winding down.

The persona welcomes every morning, for "the light keeps [his comrade's ghost] away." At night, he hears "Obscure hints of a tapping sound" and explains it away as a dream in which "A woodpecker attacks the attic beam." The woodpecker's association with Mars indicates that war memories persist long after the persona's survival of the war. His fear of ghosts and the woodpecker's relentless tapping are really manifestations of a reminding conscience. As in the other war poems, the guilt of the survivor informs this poem's imagery and movement.

The persona is of course whistling in the light, so to speak, if he thinks day brings freedom from the ghosts of the past. The insidious implication of "Morning deceived [his friend] those six years ago" is that it can deceive him as well. The final stanza reveals that the persona and his old war buddy would have little to say should they meet, except that

> . . . there will be much planting of fig trees,
> And Venus shall be clad in the prim leaf,

> And turn a solitary. And her god, forgot,
> Cast by that emblem out, shall spend his grief
> Upon us. In that day the fruit shall rot
> Unharvested. Then shall the sullen god
> Perform his mindless fury in our blood.

Suggested are the facts that war leaves solitary lovers behind and that withholding of love causes aggression. The rhetoric of the aubade waxes ironic and predicts not a day of renewal but a new day of war and destruction. The "oleander bush" of stanza three, a poisonous evergreen shrub, becomes a new and fitting emblem of the war god.

In the thirteen years between *A Summoning of Stones* and *The Hard Hours*, Hecht was to dispense with the allegorical and parabolic treatments of war in general and focus more particularly on his generation's war. The lag time before these specific treatments—between 1945, when "his unit discovered mass graves filled with thousands of charred bodies,"[31] and 1967—can apparently be accounted for by the necessity of psychological distance. There is no doubt that Hecht feels a sense of duty to "find out words / For their memorial sakes," as he says in "Persistences," from *The Venetian Vespers*. In a 1984 interview, he commented,

> The subject matter of poetry is the experience of our lives,
> both the most terrible and the most wonderful. . . . What I
> experienced in the war was not anywhere near so terrible as

having been a prisoner in one of those camps, or having died or lost a family in one. . . . Yet my sense of it is much more alive than that of the average American citizen, and I feel some- how under an obligation to not let anyone forget how terrible that was.[32]

As Hecht assimilated the war's sociological and psychopathological causes and evidences, they seemed to call for poetic utterance. An early attempt at dealing head-on with his experience, published in a 1947 issue of *The Kenyon Review*,[33] a poem titled "To a Soldier Killed in Germany," which in some of its elements resembles "A Deep Breath at Dawn," is not particulary successful. The poet seems to have experimented with several modes before hitting upon the device of setting his characters in a landscape that at once frames the subject and distances the teller from the statement's emotional impact, as the camera technique ("We move now to outside a German wood") in "'More Light! More Light!'" from *The Hard Hours* and the title "Still Life" from *Vespers* demonstrate.

CHAPTER TWO
The Hard Hours

Pressing Concerns

In 1980, Jonathan Keates called Hecht "one of the most maddeningly unprolific of contemporary poets."[1] In 1967, thirteen years after Hecht's first book, *The Hard Hours* was published, winning the Pulitzer Prize the following year. In 1971, in an interview with Gregory Fitz Gerald and William Heyen, Hecht attributed the book's success to several factors:

Heyen: Ted Hughes talks about the classical, elegant and fastidious nature of *A Summoning of Stones* as opposed to the harder, barer, more direct voice of *The Hard Hours*. Did this difference between the two books evolve naturally, or did you feel, consciously, a need for a change? Or were you perhaps reacting to criticism of your first book?

Hecht: I don't think the critics played any part in the decision. I imagine they rarely play a part in decisions poets make about their own work. Probably there were two factors. I don't want to denigrate it too much, but the first book was something like an advanced apprentice work—I was still learning my trade . . . . The subject matter, in fact, didn't have a pressing,

immediate need for me; I'd write about anything that came to
hand. In contrast, many of the poems in *The Hard Hours* are
about things that had enormous emotional importance to me; I
was prepared to attack them, whether they came out technically
perfect or not.[2]

The predominant concerns of *The Hard Hours* are Hecht's family life and his
coming to terms with his World War II experience.

The Personal Poems

Hecht's dedication of *The Hard Hours* to his sons, Jason and Adam, obliquely
acknowledges his indebtedness to classical and Judeo-Christian influences.
Significantly, Hecht's first poems were published under the diminutive "Tony,"
which he soon changed to the more classically resonant "Anthony." Fortuitously,
the great romantic love of his life is Helen, his second wife and dedicatee of his
third and fourth books.

Utilizing classical, Jewish, and Christian mythoi, "Jason" celebrates the birth of
Hecht's first son. The hyperbolic effusions of a new father dominate the poem's
rhetoric, though the sentimental exaggerations are partly moderated by humor. The
inherent sanctity of the occasion is redeemed at the close by the moving image of
a child playing war.

A series of playfully sarcastic comparisons begins the poem. To each wonder-laden question or statement, a deflatingly humorous reply or counter-statement can be surmised. The answer, for instance, to "Is it a chapel?" would be, "No, it's a hospital room."

> The room is full of gold.
> Is it a chapel? Is that the genuine buzz
> Of cherubim, the wingèd goods?
> Is it no more than sun that floods
> To pool itself at her uncovered breast?
> O lights, o numina, behold
> How we are gifted. He who never was,
> Is, and her fingers bless him and are blessed.

Are these cherubim and numina, "the wingèd goods," the real McCoy? No, they are fluorescent lights, the "genuine buzz" issuing from their weakened balancers. Is this the Virgin? No, it's the persona's wife. All of this verbal monkey business cannot detract from the truly miraculous birth, the creation *ex nihilo* expressed in the magnificent, simple line, "He who never was, / Is." The mutual exchange of love evidenced in the line, "her fingers bless him and are blessed," is Hecht's offered antidote to the world's hatred.

In the second stanza, the calm is likened to the "stillness of the seventh day" of creation. In stanza three, does the persona see Noah's Ark outside the window? No, it's Massachusetts.

> ... Slowly the ancient seas,
> Those black, predestined waters rise
> Lisping and calm before my eyes,
> And Massachusetts rises out of foam
> A state of mind in which by twos
> All beasts browse among barns and apple trees
> As in their earliest peace, and the dove comes home.

The hint at catastrophic floods and predestination injects a fatalistic air. The final stanza's touching image reminds the reader that Jason inherits the classical, Jewish, and Christian legacies of war.

> Tonight, my dear, when the moon
> Settles the radiant dust of every man,
> Powders the bedsheets and the floor
> With lightness of those gone before,
> Sleep then, and dream the story as foretold:
> Dream how a little boy alone
> With a wooden sword and the top of a garbage can
> Triumphs in gardens full of marigold.

Haunting these lines is the fact that in ancient Roman gladiatorial schools the trainees fought with wooden swords and only later graduated to more deadly instruments. By definition, the persona cannot control his son's destiny. The toy sword will transform into a gun, the garbage can lid into a bulletproof vest, the marigolds into people. In the modern era, however, the terrible, swift sword of nuclear weaponry precludes the honors and hero making that come from the hand-to-hand combat celebrated in the classical epics. In "Recalling War," Robert Graves works a similar image: "And we recall the merry ways of guns—/ . . . felling groves of trees / Like a child, dandelions with a switch!" The reverent tone of the last stanza captures the solemnity proper to miraculous births that end in sacrifice. The heroic little boy must one day join the dust of "those gone before."

"Adam" traces the unbroken line from the biblical Adam to Hecht's second son. The story of each Adam begins in harmony and ends in discord, with the present historical moment holding out hope for future restoration of the father-son accord. The first stanza imagines God speaking to the first Adam. Voiced by a God who creates by fiat, the words are capable of reification.

> "Adam, my child, my son,
> These very words you hear
> Compose the fish and starlight
> Of your untroubled dream.
> When you awake, my child,
> It shall all come true.
> Know that it was for you
> That all things were begun."

The words that compose the "fish and starlight" of Adam's dream will, when he awakens, come true, become the real and symbolic fish and stars of the Bible: Jonah's whale, the miraculous fish and loaves, the fish from which Jesus takes the tribute money, the disciples as fishers of men, and the stylized fish symbolic of Christianity; Abraham's progeny numerous as the stars of heaven, the star of David, the Magi's star, and the many symbolic stars of the book of Revelation. The poem's second stanza indicates that all parents wish for their children's dreams to materialize.

> . . . .
> And I, your father, tell
> The words over again
> As innumerable men
> From ancient times have done.

The third stanza's abrupt, fragmented opening strikes the poem's first discordant note.

> Tell them again in pain,
> And to the empty air.
> Where you are men speak
> A different mother tongue.

> Will you forget our games,
> Our hide-and-seek and song?
> Child, it will be long
> Before I see you again.

The fourth stanza contains the phrase from which the book takes its title.

> Adam, there will be
> Many hard hours,
> As an old poem says,
> Hours of loneliness.
> I cannot ease them for you;
> They are our common lot.
> During them, like as not,
> You will dream of me.

That the poet cannot ease the suffering of his loved ones is a thematic thread running through the rest of Hecht's books. The original Adam's "untroubled dream" turns into the poet's son's nightmare.

> When you are crouched away
> In a strange clothes closet

Hiding from one who's "It"
And the dark crowds in,
Do not be afraid—
O, if you can, believe
In a father's love
That you shall know some day.

The father who once played "hide-and-seek" with his son has been replaced by a stepfather "It." Or, this nightmarish scenario may contain Freudian dream imagery: Death is a pursuing "It"; the "strange . . . closet" is the coffin. The persona-father is depicted as the Father of Adam, the only One who can save him from death. The final stanza, echoing the poem's epigraph, *"Hath the rain a father? or who hath begotten the drops of dew?"* (Job 38.28), reminds the son that everything has a father.

Think of the summer rain
Or seedpearls of the mist;
Seeing the beaded leaf,
Try to remember me.
From far away
I send my blessing out
To circle the great globe.
It shall reach you yet.

The poem's incantatory power attempts to will words into reality. Just as God says to Adam, "'It *shall* all come true,'" the persona tells his Adam to believe in "a father's love / That you *shall* know some day" and that his blessing "*shall* reach you yet."

The poem's rhyme pattern mimes the movement from harmony to discord. The basic rhyme scheme of the first five stanzas is AxxxxBBA. The last stanza's end words have no rhymes within the stanza, though "me," the end word of its fourth line, repeats the end word of the *last* line of stanza four, which rhymes with the end word of the *first* line of the same stanza. Conversely, "away," the end word of the last stanza's fifth line, repeats the end word of the *first* line of stanza five, which rhymes with the end word of the *last* line of the same stanza. The purpose of this crazed symmetry is anybody's guess, though a feeble attempt might suggest it is in some way related to the magical nature accorded to words by the poem.

"The Vow" is about the child whose name should have been the poem's title. Adam, in Hecht's poem by that name, was created in the image of God. In "The Vow," the image did not "take." "The frail image of God / Lay spilled and formless." In tragic contrast to Jason's miraculous creation out of nothing ("He who never was / Is") stands the miscarried fetus, "Neither girl nor boy, / But . . . nearly my child." The unborn, spontaneously aborted fetus speaks to and comforts its mother.

> "... I am redeemed
> From pain and sorrow. Mourn rather for all
> Who breathlessly issue from the bone gates,

>   The gates of horn,
>   For truly it is best of all the fates
>   Not to be born."

Merely breathing entails pain in this world, the fetus seems to say, appealing to Sophocles' authority and offering as evidence the mother's own infancy when she nearly died of asthmatic asphixiation on Christmas Eve:

>   "Mother, a child lay gasping for bare breath
>   On Christmas Eve when Santa Claus had set
>   Death in the stocking, and the lights of death
>   Flamed in the tree. O, if you can, forget
>   You were the child, turn to my father's lips
>   Against the time
>   When his cold hand puts forth its fingertips
>   Of jointed lime."

As insurance against its parents' own deaths, the fetus advises them, to borrow Shakespeare's words, "To love that well which thou must leave ere long" (Sonnet 73). The sentiment is the same as Shakespeare's Sonnet 12: "And nothing 'gainst Time's scythe can make defense / Save breed [offspring], to brave [taunt] him when he takes thee hence." Stanza four cites the parents' improper motives as reason for their substances not cohering into a child:

> . . . And could it be
>
> That Jewish diligence and Irish jest [which]
>
> The consent of flesh and a midwinter storm
>
> Had reconciled,
>
> Was yet too bold a mixture to inform
>
> A simple child?

The poem closes with some unliteral vows, their general meaning being that the loss of the unborn will bring the living couple closer and renew their commitment to life.

It is difficult to tell pursuer from pursued in "The End of the Weekend," which may fairly be labeled the "Dover Beach" of adolescence. One way out of the dilemma is to escape between its horns by saying that the boy and girl are involved in mutual predation. The dramatic situation is straightforward. A young couple are at the boy's father's lake cabin and are about to make love when a bump in the attic serves as agent of foreplay interruptus. The poem ends with the boy's discovery of a large owl looming over a boneyard of mouse skeletons. The significance of this obviously symbolic vignette is harder to come by.[3]

By the end of the first stanza, one surmises that a sexual-economic transaction of some sort is about to occur. Note: In early Victorian England, Marryat wrote sea novels that remained boy favorites well into this century.

> A dying firelight slides along the quirt
>
> Of the cast-iron cowboy where he leans

> Against my father's books. The lariat
> Whirls into darkness. My girl, in skin-tight jeans,
> Fingers a page of Captain Marryat,
> Inviting insolent shadows to her shirt.

The rhetoric is predominantly male-centered. The cowboy and sailor images indicate men who are away from women for long periods of time, who use them when they come into town or port, and discard them for a romantic life on the free and open range or sea. The phrase "my father's books" leaves the mother conspicuously absent and indicates the father's own single, freewheeling lifestyle. "My father's books" and "My girl" further show the possessive nature of the male-oriented society that dominates or controls its environment by force of quirt and lariat. Yet the girl, "inviting insolent shadows to her shirt," knows how to play the game to her advantage.

One of the interesting areas of the poem is the white space between stanzas one and two, where the boy and girl confirm the sexual compact by words, body language, or assent of eyes. The girl's cat-like rubbing and "nails" betray her own predatory nature.

> We rise together to the second floor.
> Outside, across the lake, an endless wind
> Whips at the headstones of the dead and wails
> In the trees for all who have and have not sinned.

She rubs against me and I feel her nails.
Although we are alone, I lock the door.

The "weekend" provides a holiday from society's moral restrictions. The "end" (purpose and terminus) of the weekend implies the imminence of economic payoff, but the sexual treasure is haunted by the ghosts of ancestral sinners. In stanza three, "everything awaits / The slow unloosening of her underthings."

And then the noise. Something is dropped. It grates
Against the attic beams.
                              I climb the stairs

Armed with a belt.
                        A long magnesium strip
Of moonlight from the dormer cuts a path
Among the shattered skeletons of mice.
A great black presence beats its wings in wrath.
Above the boneyard burn its golden eyes.
Some small grey fur is pulsing in its grip.

Playing his socially determined role, our contemporary knight-cowboy takes up his belt-lariat and, in a safe act of false bravado (he knows nothing posing a real threat would be in the attic), is poised to rescue his damsel in distress by beating or tying up the assaulting dragon. Apparently, one of the couple reads the tableau of the "great black presence" over "the shattered skeletons" as a parable of sexual guilt and punishment. The incident kills the plotted for, expected dénouement, the "end" of the weekend.

Critics have disagreed about the identity of the presence, calling it an owl or bat.[4] What is more significant to the poem is the alignment of the rapacious owl, unexpectedly, with the female. The "nails" of the girl, which clutch the boy as the two ascend the stairs, are like the talons of the otherwise genderless owl: "*its* wings," "*its* golden eyes," "*its* grip."

The architectural setting begs to be victimized by Freudian interpretation. The three floors represent the superego, ego, and id. The ground floor is dominated by social norms and gender roles. In the attic resides the hidden animal. At the middle level, the ego arbitrates between the conflicting desires above and below. The poem's unresolved conclusion is puzzling, though its irresolution forces the reader to view the poem as dramatizing the vacillating desire-guilt rituals of adolescence.

In the midst of the many personal, even confessional, poems in *The Hard Hours* sits "Rites and Ceremonies," lodged like a stone in the throat. Tracing the history of the persecution and forced homelessness of the Jews, the poem impresses upon the reader the fact that there are forces in the world over which we have little if any control and which influence and sometimes dominate our lives. Several of the short personal poems that cluster on either side of the longer "Rites and Ceremonies" involve homeless individuals overtaken by hopelessness and helplessness in a world that indifferently tosses them about.

The importance of home and groundedness is brought out in "Message from the

City" and "The Letter," poems whose weaknesses reside in the cause for their genesis, a persona cut apart from his family and adrift in a relationless world.

"Message from the City" gives the feel of a person who cannot get his bearings. In free verse, the poem tries to gain balance by using spatial and temporal oppositions: "here" and "there" and "between us"; "yesterday" and "today." Self-conscious clichés ("your house, built upon sand") and a moralized landscape as setting also impede the successful transmission of the speaker's genuine pain.

"A Letter," too, resorts to cliché in its blathering confessional: "the crocus is up," "the blood goes worming," "the dark heart-root"—all of which betray what the poem's close tells, "that all is not well / With a man dead set to ignore / The endless repetitions of his own murmurous blood."

More successful is the closing poem of *The Hard Hours*, "'It Out-Herods Herod. Pray You, Avoid It,'" which clinches one of the book's major themes, that the individual is impotent to help his loved ones in the face of omnipotent and omnipresent evil, evils so immense that man has attempted, psychologically, to control them through the subliminal magic of folk tales, fairy tales, and other archetypal forms of dominance.

In stanza one, the persona's children watch a TV Western in which "with a Sunday punch, / The Good casts out the Bad." In stanza two, a poor "match-girl" in one of the children's fairy tales seals "the warty giant and witch" in a doorless jail and "strikes it rich." Stanza three depicts the persona and his wife as the "giant and witch" ready to "bust out of the clink" in which the children thought they had been sealed.

The title, from *Hamlet* (III.ii.16), comes in here. Hamlet's advice to the players is usually taken as Shakespeare's own comment on acting, that it should not be overdone. The character of Herod in medieval mystery plays was exaggerated as a ranting tyrant much loved by unsophisticated audiences. In Hecht's poem, the husband and wife overdo their parts as they argue. Each "doth protest too much."

From the historical atrocity of Herod's slaughter of the innocents, alluded to in the title, to the symbolized fears in folk and fairy tale, evil gathers momentum in the poem. The struggle between good and evil grows to metaphysical proportions. Evil personified, "Satan, bestrides the globe; / He stalks its breadth and length / And finds out even Job." A sudden tonal shift reminds the reader of a child's innocent, allegorical interpretation of mother and father and the world:

> Half God, half Santa Claus,
> But with my voice and face,
>
> A hero comes to save
> The poorman, beggarman, thief,
> And make the world behave
> And put an end to grief.

Far from being a referee in the extensive warfare between good and evil, the persona realizes his severe limitation and ultimate impotence:

> And that their sleep be sound
> I say this childermas

>   Who could not, at one time,
>   Have saved them from the gas.

Not by accident does this line fall as the final statement of *The Hard Hours*.

Modern Neuroses

A number of poems from *The Hard Hours* deal with neuroses, especially involving *idées fixes*, and emphasize modern man's fascination with the aberrant in the near and familiar, for example, the "nice boy" next door who commits mass murder.

The imagery of "Birdwatchers of America" takes advantage of the avocation of birding, and especially the linking of birds with insanity, as in the phrases "odd bird," "loony," "birdbrained," and "batty." The epigraph, taken from Baudelaire's *Journals*, speaks of "the wing of madness." In stanza one, "dove" represents the Holy Spirit and the dove of peace. The final stanza reports that "the woman next door" found a dead man when she was a child. "Rigid and bright / Upon [his] forehead, furred / With a light frost, crouched an outrageous bird." Whether this bird represents the man's insanity or his soul is not clear. The neighbors, in any case, take the story as sign of the woman's lunacy.

"Lizards and Snakes" tells of a boy who put the titular reptiles in his spinster aunt's knitting box. He is cured of his mischief on "the day / Of the big wind when you could hear the trees / Creak like rockingchairs." Aunt Martha, looking to the horizon, says, "'Sweet Jesus, please / Don't let him near me. He's as like as twins. / . . . / Look how he grins / And swinges the scaly horror of his folded tail.'" In the final line, the woman uses a phrase from Milton's "On the Morning of Christ's Nativity" to describe what is probably a tornado in the distance. Her apocalyptic hallucination is caused by the satanic imagery of her reading, the same reading that makes her treat nature allegorically and causes her inordinate fear of snakes.

"The Man Who Married Magdalene" shows that God's ambiguity is as maddening as the world's. This modernized version of the biblical story imagines Magdalene's husband spending the days after the prostitute's death in drunkenness because he cannot fathom God's mysterious and equivocal ways of meting out reward and punishment: "Stranger, here's to my wife, / Who died and went to heaven." He dreams of two angels likewise scratching their heads, one saying to the other,

> "Such as once went to Gehenna
> Now dance among the blessed.
> But Mary Magdalena,
> She had it the best."

Gehenna, the smoldering garbage dump outside Jerusalem where children were once sacrificed to the pagan Moloch, came to represent Hell. Magdalene has the best of both worlds because she has partaken of bodily pleasure and still won spiritual salvation. Thinking to take advantage of this easy formula, the husband plans "some day" to "come to in Bellevue / And make psalms unto the Lord."

In addition to looking at the deranged with curious eye, three poems explore the guilt of the powerless, the unhealthy remorse sometimes taken on by those not truly responsible for the tragedies or welfare of others.

A psychiatrist's couch is the setting of "Behold the Lilies of the Field." A man who hates his parents relates to his analyst a dream in which, as a Roman soldier, he is made to watch the torture of the emperor Valerian after his capture by the Persians.[5] Because he is unable to bear the guilt of wishing the torture of his father, his subconscious has created this dreamwork, which, instead of functioning cathartically, haunts him in his waking hours as well.

Further evidence of attempts to disguise his painful guilt are the use of the passive voice and the insistence that he is forced to watch the torture. Six times during the session, he repeats, with slight variation, "I was tied to a [phallic] post and made to watch." Ultimately, Valerian is flayed alive and his hide stuffed and hung from a (phallic) flagpole, to which "young girls were brought . . . by their mothers / To be told about the male anatomy." His dream involves an obviously displaced revenge on the effigy of his castrated father. "In the end, I was ransomed. Mother paid for me."

After his frantic relating of these events, the man's analyst asks him to rest, lean back, and "look at the flowers," whereupon he replies, "Yes. I am looking. I wish I could be like them." The title's allusion to Matthew 6.28 suggests that, like the lilies of the field, he wishes not to "toil." Like Prufrock desiring to be a pair of ragged claws, he wishes to be insensitive to the harshness of his inner and outer worlds.

"Third Avenue in Sunlight" recounts the history of John, a perpetual pariah who once "hung around the Village, / Boldly T-shirted, unfettered but unfreed." The line suggests that John is still enthralled by his own demons, or that frameless liberty causes instability, that the degree of deviation from an established and generally accepted standard is the truest measure of freedom.

John tells a stranger in the bar how as a child he played cowboys and Indians in Central Park. The childhood game matured into a "paranoid guilt about what the white men have done to the Indians, and a fear of retribution."[6] John's fear of some terrible retribution finally manifested itself in an hallucination.

. . . One summer, in Des Moines,

They entered his hotel room, tomahawks
Flashing like barracuda. He tried to pray.
Three years of treatment. Occasionally he talks
About how he almost didn't get away.

John now drowns in drink the harsh reality of his meaningless life. Just as intriguing as John's story is the persona's guilt over not helping John, really less than an acquaintance from years back. The persona has his own problems. He rationalizes: "We almost never meet. / . . . / My bar is somewhat further down the street." He has a feeling of guilt without being, in fact, responsible for John. Or is he? The poem points up the connectedness of social and personal guilt.

What the poem means aside for a moment, how the poem means is also interesting. John and the persona hide from the harsh sunlight of reality in the chiaroscuro of bars. Hecht shows the transference of John's life to his drink by shuffling the syntax of line four and replacing certain words with their synonyms in the poem's penultimate line:

       1   2   3

He <u>tilts</u> his <u>glass</u> in the <u>mild mahogany air</u>.

       3   1   2

In the <u>Rembrandt dark</u> he <u>lifts</u> his <u>amber life</u>.

The life-ruining *idée fixe* reported in "'And Can Ye Sing Baluloo When The Bairn Greets?'" is the self-loathing of an attractive woman for whom sexuality has turned disgusting. The obsession apparently began when, during "early child-hood," she discovered that her own birth was the result of her parents' sexual activity, to her an act of revolting shame.

> "I was about to be happy when the abyss
> Opened its mouth. It was empty, except for this
> Yellowish sperm of horror that glistened there.
> I tried so hard not to look as the thing grew fat

> And pulsed in its bed of hair. . . ."

Like Aunt Martha's neurosis, this woman's seems the result of puritanical beliefs about sex: "'I tried to think . . . of our swaddled link / To the Lord of Hosts, the manger, and all of that. // . . . These eyes, that many have praised as gay, / Are the stale jellies of lust in which Adam sinned.'" A sad irony is that the woman engages in an act that could be interpreted as vanity.

> "And nothing works. Sickened since God knows when,
> Since early childhood when I first saw the horror,
> I have spent hours alone before my mirror.
> There is no cure for me in the world of men."

The woman's act is instead one of self-disgust. She feels soiled, repulsive, and beyond cure. These thoughts are reported by the persona, who has a single line in the poem, the first: "All these years I have known of her despair." The woman is to him what John is to the persona of "Third Avenue in Sunlight," a broken human being who is their own *idée fixe*, but to whom they cannot or will not extend a healing hand. Their guilt seems a self-inflicted punishment for their own impotence to help someone they may not be responsible for. One of the premises of both poems is that to see or know too much about our human connections with others can be maddening.

To think too broadly or teleologically about where the individual or the human race is going may likewise be psychologically devastating, as "A Hill" attests. The event recounted in the poem could be viewed as a *déjà vu* experience, but the overwhelmingly nihilistic ambiance of the poem militates against such a reductionist interpretation. The persona even protects himself against the bleakness of the coming statement by a humorous disclaimer.

> In Italy, where this sort of thing can occur,
> I had a vision once—though you understand
> It was nothing at all like Dante's, or the vision of saints,
> And perhaps not a vision at all. . . .

Not at all like Dante's indeed, for Dante's vision was of redemption and universal purpose. By contrast, in the midst of a busy Roman street, the persona has a revelation of "a hill, mole-colored and bare" that replaces "even the great Farnese Palace itself." Ten years later, he recognizes the hill as being one with a hill "just to the left / Of the road north of Poughkeepsie," before which he stood for hours as a boy. Due to its sheer starkness, the poem defies further interpretation. It may be that after the extravagance of the world—its "books, coins, old maps, / Cheap landscapes and ugly religious prints," its "colors and noise" and "gestures of exultation"—the whole shebang may mean and come to nothing. If this be so, even the world's baseness can lay claim to a species of "godliness," as the poem claims.

Anti-Semitism as Historical Obsession

Hecht's placement of certain poems before "Rites and Ceremonies" is calculated to give added resonance to the images or quotations which are sprinkled like tesserae throughout the long poem. To cite but one instance here, the epigraph to "Adam"—"Hath the rain a father? or who hath begotten the drops of dew?"—is echoed in "Who / Fathered the fathering rain," from "Rites."

"Tarantula or The Dance of Death," a vignette of plague-time medieval Europe, prepares the reader for Section II of "Rites," entitled "The Fire Sermon," which recounts the ritual persecution of the Jews who, during the fourteenth century, were suspected of causing the epidemic by poisoning public wells.

Apart from its connection with "Rites and Ceremonies," "Tarantula" seems out of place in *The Hard Hours*, partly because of its personification and use of the Black Death as its speaker. Several anachronisms, especially "democrat" and the implied tarantella and *danse macabre* of the title, contribute to the feel of Death's omnipresence and omnipotence. The poem opens, "During the plague I came into my own." In monarchical Europe, the Black Death "comes into his own," becomes the newest tyrant, and "comes into" the bodies of His constituents. No respecter of persons, the bubonic representative of the great Leveler is depicted as a demagogue who brings no redeeming social changes to offset his "abuse." "The blind head of bone / Grinned its abuse // Like a good democrat at everyone." The etymology of "democrat" (power of the people) heightens the irony of the poem's penultimate sentence, "Moreover, flame / Is powerless against contagion."

The spasms of the dying victim constitute the subtitle's dance of death, an allegorical treatment of Death first appearing in the theater and art of the fourteenth century as a result of widespread disease. Throughout the poem, hard rhymes combine with clever idioms to emphasize Death's taunting malice.

> But the most curious part of it is the dance.
> The victim goes, in short, out of his head.
>> A sort of trance
>
> Glazes the eyes, and then the muscles take
> His will away from him, the legs begin
> Their funeral jig, the arms and belly shake
>> Like souls in sin.

The convulsions resemble those thought to have been brought on by the bite of a tarantula. Tarantism was "a hysterical malady, characterized by an extreme impulse to dance, which prevailed as an epidemic in . . . Italy from the 15th to the 17th century, popularly attributed to the bite or 'sting' of the tarantula." Hecht's title makes self-conscious use of "tarantula," which is often erroneous for "tarantella," "a rapid whirling South Italian dance popular with the peasantry since the fifteenth century, when it was supposed to be the sovereign remedy for tarantism."[7]

Though the designation "Black Death" is not used in the poem, it seems clear that the speaker is the personified plague because of the symptoms (fever and dark spots), remedies mentioned (runes, charms, smoke-pots in the house), and the suggestive last sentence, "That was the *black* winter when I came / Into my own" (italics added).

"Rites and Ceremonies" is a poem whose driving force is doubt, fueled by an incredible will to believe. The title suggests that persecution of Jews resembles periodic ritual sacrifices and indicates psychological needs in the oppressors rather than inherent faults in their victims. The formal stanzas themselves partake of ritual by containing while expressing powerful emotions.[8] Like *The Wasteland*, to which "Rites" has been compared, the poem is a gold mine of allusions. Nearly every line can be glossed, but only to a certain point does such myopic hounding out of references pay back in accrued meaning.[9]

The epic begins in the present, reviews the past suffering of the Hebrews, and closes by seeking peace with its own bitterness. Section I, "The Room," records the cruel treatment of the Jews during World War II. Section II, "The Fire Sermon," casts a cold eye on the use of Jews as scapegoats during the Middle Ages. Section III, "The Dream," dramatizes their persecution into the late sixteenth century. After these voyages into the underworld of human nature, Section IV, "Words for the Day of Atonement," resurfaces in the present to show that modern man has not shed the barbarity of his ancestors. Remarkably, the last section, voicing a belief that transcends (without ignoring) empirical evidence, turns snakes into flowers. Originally at odds with his Creator, the persona ends "at one" with Him, as the etymology of "atone" adumbrates.

In the last of the poem's four sections, the persona asks,

And to what purpose, as the darkness closes about

And the child screams in the jellied fire,

Had best be our present concern,

Here, in this wilderness of comfort

In which we dwell.

America is portrayed as a "wilderness of comfort," not the promised land of the perennially homeless Jews. Mention has been made that Hecht "sets up" several passages in "Rites" with thematically related poems that serve almost as prologues to the longer poem without, however, losing their identity as independent constructions. A loose translation of a sonnet by Du Bellay, entitled "Heureux Qui, Comme Ulysse, A Fait un Beau Voyage," immediately precedes "Rites." Du Bellay's title seems to prophesy an epic journey by the Jews before returning to their homeland. Section III of "Rites" draws on the poem that precedes it: "Du Bellay, poet, take no thought of them; / And yet they too are exiles. . . ." Unlike the homesick Du Bellay and the Jews, the persona has enjoyed a homecoming. "I have come home" from the war, he says in Section I.

Given the suffering of the Jews, the persona hopes to find its cause, its purpose, and some sense of justice, perhaps even a hearty Old Testament vengeance. The poem refers in several places to Psalm 8, whose first lines inform the poem's movement and provide not a little irony:

O Lord our Lord, how excellent is thy name in all the
earth! who hast set thy glory above the heavens.

Out of the mouth of babes and sucklings hast thou

ordained strength because of thine enemies, that thou

mightest still the enemy and the avenger.

When I consider thy heavens, the work of thy fingers,

the moon and the stars, which thou hast ordained;

What is man, that thou art mindful of him?

The last line above assumes that God is mindful of man, but the persona is constantly amazed by His noncommittal stance in the face of pain, especially that of children. Knowing he is ultimately powerless to redeem Jewish suffering, the poet finds solace in building a monument to their history. In "Persistences," from *The Venetian Vespers*, Hecht likens "huge helices of snow" fallen outside his window to the numberless Jews killed in World War II.

Those throngs disdain to answer,

Though numberless as flakes;

Mine is the task to find out words

For their memorial sakes

Who press in dense approaches,

Blue numeral tattoos

Writ crosswise on their arteries,

The burning, voiceless Jews.

"Rites," more than an irritable seeking after fact and reason, is a memorial to the suffering of the Jews and a record of the poet's own awe at their persistent faith.

The opening stanza of "Rites" begins with a lovely psalmic tone that turns bitterly ironic at its close.

> . . . .
>
> Furnisher, hinger of heaven, who bound
> > the lovely Pleaides,
>
> . . . .
>
> Lord, who, governing cloud and waterspout,
> > o my King,
> held me alive till this my forty-third year—
> > *in whom we doubt—*
> Who was that child of whom they tell
> > in lauds and threnes?
> whose holy name all shall pronounce
> > Emmanuel,
> which being interpreted means,
> > *"Gott mit uns"*?

Some of the devices and rhetoric imitate Swinburne and Hopkins, and the "forty-third year" is decidedly Whitmanesque ("Song of Myself," 1: "I, now thirty-seven years old"). This agnostic prayer, especially its closing *"Gott mit uns,"* approaches blasphemy, as does a reference to the German "Iron Cross" a few lines later, as do several ironic questions throughout the poem, to cite a single example, "Are the vents in the ceiling, Father, to let the spirit depart?" Yet the persona's sarcasm is tempered by compassion.

At the end of stanza four, Hecht cites a peaceful line from what is considered by many to be the most beautiful German poem: *"Die Vögelein schweigen im Walde."* From Goethe's *"Wanderers Nachtlied,"* the line is poetically translated by Long-fellow, "The birds are asleep in the trees," and by John Rothensteiner, "The birds in the forest are sleeping," but a literal rendering, "The birds are silent in the forest," more accurately contrasts the horrors of the Holocaust recounted in the remainder of the sentence to which it is connected, the rift between the tranquil present and strident past amplified by a stanza break:

> But for years the screaming continued, night and day,
> And the little children were suffered to come along, too.
> At night, Father, in the dark, when I pray,
> I am there, I am there. I am pushed through
> With the others to the strange room
> Without windows; whitewashed walls, cement floor.
> Millions, Father, millions have come to this pass,
> Which a great church has voted to "deplore."

The first sentence echoes Matthew 19.14, "But Jesus said, Suffer little children, and forbid them not, to come to me." Hecht again uses the Whitmanesque pose, "I am there" ("Song of Myself," 33: "I am the man, I suffer'd, I was there"), in order to give the scene immediacy and vividness.[10] The last word of the stanza, "deplore," is derived from the Latin *plorare*, "to wail," used four lines later in a parallel position to call attention to the irony:

> We are crowded in here naked, female and male.
> An old man is saying a prayer. And now we start
> To panic, to claw at each other, to wail
> As the rubber-edged door closes on chance and choice.

In the first line, the gas chamber becomes an ironic ark, its salvific implication reversed.

In Section II, the event recounted takes on archetypal significance. The survivors of a decimating plague during the Middle Ages wonder, "Was it a judgment?":

> Among the heathen, the king of Tharsis, seeing
> Such sudden slaughter of his people, began a journey to Avignon
> With a great multitude of his nobles, to propose to the pope
> That he become a Christian and be baptized,
> Thinking that he might assuage the anger of God
> Upon his people for their wicked unbelief.

> But when he had journeyed twenty days,
>
> He heard the pestilence had struck among the Christians
>
> As among other peoples. So, turning in his tracks,
>
> He travelled no farther, but hastened to return home.
>
> The Christians, pursuing these people from behind,
>
> Slew about seven thousand of them.

A large number of people suffer for no apparent reason. Mircea Eliade, in *The Myth of the Eternal Return,* explains that primitive peoples were able to endure suffering as long as it "seemed neither gratuitous nor arbitrary."[11]

> The primitive who sees his field laid waste by drought, . . . his child ill, himself unlucky as a hunter, knows that all these contingencies are not due to chance but to certain magical or demonic influences, against which the priest or sorcerer possesses weapons.[12]

The incident related by Hecht follows the archetypal paradigm: there is an unexplained plague, and the king of Tharsis, representing the community, turns to the sorcerer, the pope, "to make the gods favorable to him," as Eliade says, or to "assuage the anger of God," as the poem reads.

"Tarantula" and its subtitle, "The Dance of Death," clarify "the foxtrot of death" and "the dancing master's foot" of Section II as puns on the dance of death and a rat's foot, rats and fleas being the major transporters of the bubonic plague. The Europeans in this section seek a determinant for their misfortunes and wonder if God has judged them for some misdeed. When they see that innocent children, "the meek and the faithful," sheep, and even Friars Minor and Friars Preachers are not exempt from the plague, they fabricate a cause: "And presently it was found to be / Not a judgment."

> For the evidence now was in: in Berne, under torture,
> Two Jews had confessed to poisoning the wells.
> Wherefore throughout Europe were these platforms erected,
> Even as here in the city of Strasbourg,
> And the Jews assembled upon them,
> Children and all, and tied together with rope.

The Jews are to be burned as scapegoats for the afflicted people. In the span of four lines, "two Jews," their confession obtained under torture, become "the Jews." Again, Eliade:

> The primitive . . . cannot conceive of an unprovoked suffering;
> it arises from a personal fault . . . or from his neighbor's
> malevolence . . .; but there is always a fault at the bottom of

it. . . . . In each case, the suffering becomes intelligible and hence tolerable.[13]

While the attempted genocide failed as cure for the disease, it must have been psychologically comforting. Northrop Frye explains that in ritual

> we see . . . an imitation of nature which has a strong element of
> what we call magic in it. Magic seems to begin as something
> of a voluntary effort to recapture a lost rapport with the natural
> cycle. This sense of a deliberate recapturing of something no
> longer possessed is a distinctive mark of human ritual. . . . But
> the impetus of the magical element in ritual is clearly toward a
> universe in which a stupid and indifferent nature is no longer
> the container of human society, but is contained by that society,
> and must rain or shine at the pleasure of man.[14]

The principle applies to the situation in "Rites." There is a "lost rapport with the natural cycle" because of the plague, and the people locate and isolate the cause in the Jewish people, from whom they plan to expel the evil by fire. If they can kill the Jews, the natural cycle will be reestablished.

Section III contains another example of the Jews' role as ritual scapegoats. The setting is "the first Saturday in Carnival." "Yesterday it was acrobats, and a play / About Venetian magnificos, and in the interval / Bull-baiting, palm-reading, juggling, but today / The race," to be run down a mile-long gauntlet of drunken, fun-loving, sadistic young couples. "The men have whips and sticks with bunting tied / About them," the bunting symbolizing their pleasure at inflicting pain. First through the gauntlet are camels, horses, and asses. A group of young men is to follow.

> Twenty young men, naked, except the band
> Around their loins, wait for the horn's command.
> Christ's Vicar chose them, and imposed his fine.
>
> Du Bellay, poet, take no thought of them;
> And yet they too are exiles. . . .

Associated with animals, the Jews are also suprahuman, Christlike. Christ suffered vicariously for humans, the Pope is Christ's "Vicar" or substitute on earth, and the Jews here, by dictate of "Christ's Vicar," are buffeted as Christ was on the Golgotha road and vicariously pay for the sins their tormentors have committed in the year preceding the Carnival season. Eliade states that "every ritual has a divine model, an archetype."

Readers familiar with ethnography and the history of re-
ligions are well aware of the importance of a whole series of
periodic ceremonies, which, for convenience, we can group
under two main headings: (1) annual expulsion of demons,
diseases, and sins; (2) rituals of the days preceding and following the New Year.[15]

In "Rites," the purification via substitute sufferer takes place at the beginning of the
spiritual New Year and has biblical precedent in the Flood, Sodom and Gomorrah,
and other similarly destructive cleansings.

Section IV compares the twentieth-century Jewish exile not to a desert but to a
degraded urban wilderness. "And again we wander the wilderness / For our
transgressions / Which are confessed in the daily papers." The plea in the fifth
stanza of the section relies for its incantatory strength on biblical definitions such
as "His name is Wonderful" and "His name is Just."

We come before thee relying on thy name;
O deal with us according to thy name;
For the sake of the glory of thy name;
As the gracious and merciful God is thy name.

The stanza hearkens back to "Emmanuel" of the poem's first stanza, "which being interpreted means, / *'Gott mit uns.'"* The irony of the German phrase now purged, the persona asks God to deal with his people as if He were in fact among them. The penultimate stanza is a prayer for the protection of

> The saved and saving remnant, the promised third,
>> Who in a later day
> When we again are compassed about with foes,
> Shall be for us a nail in thy holy place
> There to abide according to thy word.

"Saved," they are also the "saving remnant, the promised third" (Zechariah 13.8-9) because God has promised to answer their prayers, one of which figures in the last stanza. The above passage claims this remnant's messianic function for the remainder of Israel, since they "Shall be for us a nail in thy holy place." Compare Ezra 9.8, "And now for a little space grace hath been shewed from the Lord our God, to leave us a remnant to escape, and to give us a nail in his holy place, that our God may lighten our eyes, and give us a little reviving in our bondage." Throughout history, from the "remnant" to Christ to the Holocaust victims, the Jews have appropriated racial meaning by seeing themselves as worthy sacrifices for the salvation of others.

The concluding stanza indicates that there will be another, perhaps final, persecution, but these latter-day Jews, like Shadrach, Meshach, and Abed-nego, will be unharmed by the fires.

> Neither shall the flame
> Kindle upon them, nor the fire burn
> A hair of them, for they
> Shall be thy care when it shall come to pass,
> And calling on thy name
> In the hot kilns and ovens, they shall turn
> To thee as it is prophesied, and say,
> *"He shall come down like rain upon mown grass."*

Zechariah 13.9 reads, "And I will bring the third part through the fire, and will refine them as silver is refined, and will try them as gold is tried: they shall call on my name, and I will hear them: I will say, It is my people: and they shall say, The Lord is my God."

In the chapter "Misfortune and History," subheaded "History Regarded as Theophany," Eliade says, "It may . . . be said with truth that the Hebrews were the first to discover the meaning of history as the epiphany of God. . . ." This view others have called *Heilsgeschichte*, "salvation history," history as the record of God's progressive revelation of Himself to His people or to all people. Whether or not this belief is true, the defense mechanism is not made ineffectual: "only one fact counts: by virtue of this view tens of millions of men were able, for century after century, to endure great historical pressures without despairing, without committing suicide or falling into that spiritual aridity that always brings with it a relativistic or nihilistic view of history."[16]

The Jews have accomodated the tragic facts of their experience by creating an overseeing God and a precedential written history whose value cannot be overestimated. Doubtless, there is comfort in reciting, "Yea, for thy sake are we killed all the day long; we are counted as sheep for the slaughter" (Psalm 44.22). Through the recitation of numerous similar passages, Jews and Christians have imbued and ennobled their suffering with the accolade of privilege.

In "'More Light! More Light!,'" Hecht's bleakest poem about human nature, it is difficult to assess which of the participants in the parody of sacrifice is most despicable. Much of the poem's irony turns on Goethe's deathbed cry for more light.

The first two stanzas, Daniel Hoffman claims, describe "the burning at the stake of an accused heretic in the Middle Ages."[17] At this point, the poem has a strongly anti-theodicy flavor. "His legs were blistered sticks on which the black sap / Bubbled and burst as he howled for the Kindly Light." The torturers' absence of compassion in the face of extreme anguish ("And that was but one, and by no means one of the worst") is emphasized by the matter-of-fact, scene-shifting eye of a camera.

> We move now to outside a German wood.
> Three men are there commanded to dig a hole
> In which the two Jews are ordered to lie down
> And be buried alive by the third, who is a Pole.
>
> Not light from the shrine at Weimar beyond the hill
> Nor light from heaven appeared. But he did refuse.

> A Lüger settled back deeply in its glove.
>
> He was ordered to change places with the Jews.

Hoffman says, "In the absence of the light of either Goethe's humanism or the Word, the Pole's refusal may suggest that he, like their Nazi captor, is too scornful of Jews to kill them himself."[18] "Not light" and "Nor light" do seem to negate the title's double plea for more light, but the Pole's attempted sacrificial act, miming Christ's, dictates another reading. Contrary to expectation, the Jews, because "Much casual death had drained away their souls," bury to his "quivering chin" their momentary savior and are ordered "To dig him out again and to get back in," that is, to resurrect him.

The poem implies that sacrifice involves a reciprocal exchange, its efficacy dependent, on one side of the equation, upon a person committing the sacrificial act and, on the other, someone accepting its redemptive consequence for himself. The poem is about the failure of sacrifice when this mutuality is absent or retracted. The Lüger hovering over both parties engaged in the sacrificial formula assures that the sacrifice would in any case have amounted to little more, in the immediate moment, than a courteous gesture preceding the death of both parties. Instead of following the christological pattern of death, burial, and resurrection, the Pole is first buried, then resurrected, then shot, his wound reminiscent of Christ's.

> No light, no light in the blue Polish eye.
>
> When he finished a riding boot packed down the earth.

> The Lüger hovered lightly in its glove.
>
> He was shot in the belly and in three hours bled to death.

Instead of rising after three days, he bleeds to death in three hours. "No light, no light" again negates the plea for "More Light" from the "Kindly Light." Synechdoche emphasizes the impersonality of the ritual. The Nazi is depicted only as a "Lüger," "glove," and "riding boot." The Pole is referred to as a "chin," a "head," a "blue Polish eye," and a "belly."

Unlike the Jews in "Rites and Ceremonies," the Jews in "'More Light!'" lose, in the existential confrontation with death, their identity as Jews, what Eliade calls their "historical consciousness."[19] As a consequence, they break one of their God's highest laws, the commandment not to kill. The poem's final lines, in which ashes issuing from the smokestacks of extermination factories settle upon the Polish "eyes in a black soot," suggest that the light of compassion must come from within each person, not from a transcendent Being whom humans wish would control destiny or impart understanding of tragic or absurd events.

In 1986, Brad Leithauser, in his ominously titled essay "Poet for a Dark Age," said that "A plausible case could be made that [Hecht's] four books. . . record a journey from darkness into greater darkness; certainly, *The Venetian Vespers* is a very dark book indeed."[20] Without denying this general tendency in Hecht's verse, I would argue that *The Hard Hours* had a purgative effect on Hecht's thought, so that *Millions of Strange Shadows* has more light moments than all of the books together. In it, Hecht gets away from the stricter historicity of *Hours* and returns to the metaphysical speculativeness and verbal playfulness of *A Summoning of Stones*.

CHAPTER THREE

Millions of Strange Shadows

"All That Ancient Pain"

After the elaborate forms of *A Summoning of Stones* and the looser poems of *The Hard Hours*, Hecht seems, in *Millions of Strange Shadows*, to have settled into the verse strategy he is most comfortable with, one he seems to have been tending towards all along.

Part of chapter one dealt with Hecht's use of paintings and tableaux in his meditative poems. The structural design of describing a painting and tracing the thoughts it evokes is clearly evinced in poems from *Stones* such as "The Place of Pain in the Universe," "A Poem for Julia," and "At the Frick." The forms of these poems, however, are not affected by the styles of the paintings described. In several poems from *Shadows*, a transference of form flowing from painting to poem is detectable.

Poets frequently employ historical settings to show the insignificance of the individual awash in the Sturm und Drang of modern life, but, throughout *Shadows*, Hecht "give[s] breath back to the past"[1] in order to stress the importance of the present and to provide both positive and negative models for contemporary society. In "A Birthday Poem," he not only translates painting techniques into poetics but delivers a running commentary on the advantages of using the Flemish strategies to focus on his subject, to place his subject in a meaningful historical context, and thus to contrast vast historical expanses with the (decidedly favored) vignettes of personal relationships. Historical events serve as the backdrop for the poem's foreground or major subject, the wife whose birthday occasions the poem.

The twelve sestets may be divided into three movements: five stanzas discourse on spatial distance, two on temporal distance, and five expound on, while giving personal ramifications of, distances in both space and time. The setting is a sunny noon, the June 22, 1976 birthday of Hecht's wife.

> Like a small cloud, like a little hovering ghost
> > Without substance or edges,
> Like a crowd of numbered dots in a sick child's puzzle,
> > A loose community of midges
> Sways in the carven shafts of noon. . . .

The poem begins in a manner typical of Hecht's other meditative poems: he sees an object or muses on a holiday, which leads him to further reflections on the object or social custom. Here, a cloud of midges leads the persona first to various analogies then to observations on optics:

> Intent upon such tiny copter flights,
> > The eye adjusts its focus
> To those billowings about ten feet away,
> > That hazy, woven hocus-pocus
> Or shell game of air, whose casual sleights

Leave us unable certainly to say

What lies behind it, or what sets it off
    With fine diminishings,
Like the pale towns Mantegna chose to place
    Beyond the thieves and King of Kings. . . .

When "the eye adjusts its focus" to a cloud ten feet away, we are "unable certainly to say / What lies behind it" because when the eye focuses on one object, those behind and before it are blurred, racked out of focus. The persona observes that this was Mantegna's technique, to attempt to translate the optics of the eye unchanged onto the canvas. The persona returns to the midges, now calling them motes:

And we know it would take an act of will
    Plus a firm, inquiring squint
To ignore those drunken motes and concentrate
    On the blurred, unfathomed background tint
Of deep sea-green Holbein employed to fill
The space behind his ministers of state,

As if one range slyly obscured the other.
    As, in the main, it does.
All of our Flemish distances disclose

A clarity that never was:

Dwarf pilgrims in the green faubourgs of Mother

And Son, stunted cathedrals, shrunken cows.

Through intense concentration, we can "ignore those drunken motes" and notice the background, but we cannot bring it into focus without losing focus on the midges: "one range slyly obscure[s] the other." Mantegna and Holbein feature central figures by depicting them in focus in the foreground and by setting them against a background "employed [merely] to fill / . . . space." They create the illusion of distance by using diminishing proportion and diminishing line clarity towards the vanishing point and by using progressively muted colors towards the horizon (the "fine diminishings" of line 14), thus creating a stronger emphasis on the central figures than if everything were in sharp focus, as in photographs with infinite depth of field.

The Flemish paintings differ from the Italian and German of roughly the same period (represented by Mantegna and Holbein) in that most do bring all the planes into focus. First, many do not use "fine diminishings" of color to show depth but give background colors the same tonal qualities as those in the foreground. Brueghel's paintings, notably *The Peasant Wedding*, exemplify this Flemish technique. Second, many use a type of perspective which gives not so much the effect of distance as of collage, as in Memling's panorama *The Passion of Christ*. To depict the major events of Christ's life, Memling condensed time and space. To one not familiar with the two-dimensional depiction of a sequence of events in narrative painting, the effect seems to be of simultaneity in time, not of time and event unfolding. In many Flemish paintings of this sort, the depths between the planes (often on an ascending, winding road) have been contracted, and the characters do not diminish in size as they approach the "back" (and top) of the scene. Third, most Flemish paintings do not accurately depict atmospheric changes from foreground to background. Sometimes, the atmosphere is clear from front to back. Most often, the haze of distance is shown only in the remotest perspectives, as in Jan van Eyck's *The Madonna of the Chancellor Rolin* and Roger van der Weyden's *Crucifixion*.

In adopting these three qualities of Flemish narrative painting—consistency of color quality from fore- to background, the omission of segments of depth, and the lack of atmospheric changes—to his poetry, Hecht gives his wife (as a child in the photograph and as a woman on her present birthday) a "clarity that never was" (as line 28 says of Flemish paintings) and thereby gives her an importance that never was. He has created, in short, a new type of hyperbole. Hecht adopts the Flemish techniques in the following manner: analogous to consistency of color quality from fore- to background and to the lack of atmospheric changes are the characters in the fore- and background, who are drawn with equal vividness, so that it is not easy to tell what the poem "is about" until the closing few lines; analogous to the omission of segments of depth are Hecht's sudden leaps, without warning or transition, from the past to the present.

The distortions of the Flemish style are quite noticeable in Hugo van der Goes' *Portinari Altarpiece* and in Hans Memling's panels on *The Shrine of St. Ursula*, which contain "dwarf pilgrims / . . . stunted cathedrals, [and] shrunken cows," as the persona of "A Birthday Poem" says. Hecht's implementation of the technique causes analogous distortions, these being the very reason he makes the translation.

In *The Last Flowering of the Middle Ages*, Joseph van der Elst says,

> In van der Weyden's *Christ on the Cross* . . . the city in the
> background seems to push and pull for its position in the third
> dimension. But as a surface pattern of composition it is exactly
> the right size to catch the observer's interest and give an idea of
> the relative importance of all the elements in the design.[2]

A painter can show the important figure by placing that figure at the center of the canvas, or at the center of attention, as in van der Goes' *The Adoration of the Shepherds*, from the Portinari Altar. In translating the visual immediacy of two-dimensional painting techniques into the linear unfolding of words in a poem, the major problem is how to highlight the central figure. Hecht generally indicates the focal figure (1) in his titles, (2) by internal hints, and/or (3) by placement of the figure in the last stanzas. This latter method forces the reader to see the focal figure in perspective: the historical background of the early stanzas in "A Birthday Poem" has relative importance, the wife (in the latter stanzas, but foremost in the persona's mind) ultimate importance. The major figure is rarely allotted the most space in numbers of words or stanzas, and in "A Poem for Julia," from *Stones*, Julia is never mentioned. What van der Elst calls "the relative importance of all the elements in the design" is the theme of the second movement of "A Birthday Poem":

> It's the same with Time. Looked at *sub specie*
> *Aeternitatis*, from

The snow-line of some Ararat of years,
  Scholars remark those kingdoms come
To nothing, to grief, without the least display
Of anything so underbred as tears,

And with their Zeiss binoculars descry
    Verduns and Waterloos,
The man-made mushroom's deathly overplus,
  Caesars and heretics and Jews
Gone down in blood, without batting an eye,
As if all history were deciduous.

Strength of emotion is diluted or lost altogether when viewed from sufficient distance. The cyclical or repetitive nature of history presented in *Hours*, especially of Jewish history in "Rites and Ceremonies," is reiterated in the fine analogy "as if all history were deciduous."[3]

Hecht's theme of the importance of personal lives in juxtaposition with grandiose historical events is dramatized pictorially by Brueghel's *Fall of Icarus* and poetically by Auden's "Musée des Beaux Arts." The basic components of Auden's poem:

About suffering they were never wrong,
The Old Masters: how well they understood

Its human position; how it takes place

While someone else is eating or opening a window

. . . .

In Brueghel's *Icarus*, for instance: how everything turns away

Quite leisurely from the disaster; . . .

. . . .

. . . the expensive delicate ship that must have seen

Something amazing, a boy falling out of the sky,

Had somewhere to get to and sailed calmly on.

The movement in Auden's poem from abstract statement to specific illustration is the same informing structure in Hecht's "The Feast of Stephen," "The Odds," "Going the Rounds," and "'Gladness of the Best,'" with the difference that Hecht imitates the general style of the Flemish masters while Auden appropriated the theme only, and of a single painting. A cousin to Hecht's and Auden's attempts is William Carlos Williams' "The Dance," which imitates the rhythms of the dance in Brueghel's The *Kermess*, also known as *Peasants Dancing*. The poem's dactyls break down in the middle lines to imitate the stumbling of the drunken peasants.

In the first movement of "A Birthday Poem," the persona sees midges from ten feet. In the second, scholars view history from a great temporal distance and assign humans no more importance than a cloud of bugs. In the third, Hecht gives the contrasting views personal application: when we see, with historical consciousness, those who are close to us in space and time, we experience a shocking realization.

It's when we come to shift the gears of tense
That suddenly we note
A curious excitement of the heart
And slight catch in the throat:—
When, for example, from the confluence
That bears all things away I set apart

The inexpressible lineaments of your face,
Both as I know it now,
By heart, by sight, by reverent touch and study,
And as it once was years ago,
Back in some inaccessible time and place,
Fixed in the vanished camera of somebody.

You are four years old here in this photograph.
You are turned out in style,
In a pair of bright red sneakers, a birthday gift.

In the present tense of the poem, the persona is near his wife in space and time; in the "vanished" moment of her childhood, captured in the photograph, he is distant from her in space and time. Seeing these two points from the distant vantage of "the confluence / That bears all things away" (from the present flowing into the past), he experiences a "catch in the throat," a reminder of death. That "the sneakers' red / Has washed away in acids" suggests that Time will likewise blanch the flush from her cheeks.

In the penultimate stanza, the persona again shifts "the gears of tense." What is near, he views from the distance of future time—he realizes that the passing of the same number of birthdays between the photo and the present may well bring his wife's death; and what is distant (Shakespeare's voice), he hears as if it were close:

> . . . A voice is spent,
> Echoing down the ages in my head:
> *What is your substance, whereof are you made,*
> *That millions of strange shadows on you tend?*

The persona realizes not only that insubstantial though cherished appearances, such as his wife's face, reside in transitory space and time, but also that an enduring essence may transcend the worldly flux that causes our loves to age and die. This metaphysical trade-off, however, gives him little solace.

> O my most dear, I know the live imprint
> Of that smile of gratitude,
> . . . .
> O that I may be worthy of that look.

Knowing he will not share her companionship forever, the persona is moved to adoration tinctured with pathos. The last stanza is similar in effect to that of "Dover

Beach": "Ah, love, let us be true / To one another!"

In "Going the Rounds: A Sort of Love Poem," love's wheel of fortune has turned. Hecht uses one aspect of painting (or photographic) technique to broach his poem's subject, the vicissitudes of love. As in *Hours*, Hecht continues to emphasize that personal, intimate relationships upstage the impersonal backdrop of history against which they are acted out.

The first section of "Going the Rounds" presents a general, historical background while the second paints the foreground, the more important view to the speaker, who recognizes in Section II that the general axioms of Fate are nonetheless applicable to his particular life. Within the general movement of Section I, there are subdivisions in which Hecht paints what he terms in stanza six a "moralized landscape" (*cf.* the French *paysage moralisé*) whose events or scenes have bearing on his persona's specific situation.

Section I consists of three minor movements of two stanzas each. Despite the "leaps" between each subsection, a clear and relentless logical progression is evident. The first two stanzas, comprising the first minor movement, speak of dizzying heights. The second minor movement draws an analogy between physical and spiritual heights ("And there are heights of spirit. / And one of these is love") and wonders whether Fortuna's fatal principles apply to the spiritual heights of love as gravity applies impartially to all physical bodies: "And, as I must, / I acknowledge on this high rise / The ancient metaphysical distrust," which the persona earlier interprets as the fear engendered by all the warnings of Fortuna: "'What goes up must come down.'" In the third minor movement, the speaker defies Fortuna. Though "That goddess is remorseless," he wishes his love to know "I love you, know that you are most dear / To one who seeks to know / How, for your sake, to confront his pride and fear." The gesture is selfless, but pride, deadliest of sins, is present—and, as everyone knows, pride goeth before a fall. The moralizings, ironically his own, seem distant to his situation. The "homily on Fate" (spun by himself) and the lessons of "The Life of More" and "A Mirror For Magistrates," from stanzas one and two, seem not to apply to him personally.

Then the "painting" of the poem shifts suddenly to the foreground of Section II. His fall comes abruptly, his appropriately blunt words accentuating the irony and surprise.

> No sooner have the words got past my lips—
> (I exaggerate for effect)
> But two months later you have packed your grips
> And left. And left eye-shadow, Kotex, bra,
> A blue silk slip-dress that I helped select,
> And Fortuna shouts, "Hurrah!"

Two stanzas later, he continues.

> And what am I to say? "Well, at least it will do
> For a poem."? From way down here,
> The Guy in the Lake, I gaze at the distant blue
> Beyond the surface, and twice as far away.
> Deep in the mirror, I am reversed but clear.

The persona realizes he is not immune to fate. Likened to Narcissus, he sees himself as a candidate for inclusion in *A Mirror for Magistrates*, a moral work about the tragic fall of great English personages intended to teach contemporary rulers the lessons of history so as not to repeat them. The next stanza clarifies the reason for Section I, the background.

> Sackville would smile. Well, let him smile. To say
> Nothing about those girls
> I turned into wood, like Daphne. And every day
> Cavendish mutters about his Cardinal, scorned
> Son-of-a-butcher. More God damn moral pearls.

Sackville wrote the *Induction* to the 1563 edition of the *Mirror*. The *Dictionary of National Biography* reports that George Cavendish, "gentle-man-usher" of Cardinal Wolsey ("'an honest poor man's son'—report said, son of a butcher"), "laid to heart the lesson of Wolsey's fall, and eschewed ambition." Cavendish also wrote poems "after the fashion of the 'Mirrour for Magistrates'" which "represent the lamentations of fallen favourites bemoaning their errors."

After this stanza, the speaker's self-flagellation ceases. He may not believe in Fortuna, but he sees the truth symbolized by her Wheel. These abstract moralizings, however, offer no comfort, for his personal relationship with the woman is of paramount importance to him. If Fate has forced him to pay for his pride, perhaps some other type of Justice will allow him to pay another outstanding debt.

These deeps remind me we are still not square.
A fog thickens into cold smoke. Perhaps
You too will remember the terror of that place,
    The breakers' dead collapse,

The cry of the boy, pulled out by the undertow,
    Growing dimmer and more wild,
And how, the dark currents sucking from below,
When I was not your lover or you my wife,
Yourself exhausted and six months big with child,
    You saved my son's life.

The speaker finds solace in the fact that, despite the relationship's bitter ending, the woman has left him a more meaningful remembrancer than her intimate accoutrements—his son.

    The poem's foreground and background are balanced: they are allotted six stanzas each; everything included in the background is relevant to the foreground; the tertiary movement of the background has the efficiency of a syllogism. Van der Elst said of Weyden's *Christ on the Cross*, "Landscape is a factor of scale against which to judge the size of the foreground figures."[4] Applying this statement as touchstone, we can see that the speaker is presumptuous to assume he is more important than More, Sackville, or Cavendish, yet one of Hecht's primary uses of history is to emphasize that contemporaries are more important than dead historical figures, who may nevertheless serve as positive or negative models for the living. What the persona understates is the very theme of *The Mirror For Magistrates*, that one's moral flaws, not the fabricated whimsy of fortune, precipitate one's downfall.

In "The Cost," the first poem of *Shadows*, Hecht both asserts the primacy of the individual and acknowledges the value of history. The first two stanzas, a meditation on balance and centrifugal force, serve to introduce the actual background and foreground, which are alternately flipped as if to show the opposite sides of a coin.

The foreground is composed of a young Italian couple on a motorcycle; the Dacian Wars comprise the background. The two planes alternate and then interweave, racking between the young Italians on the motorcycle and the Italian recruits and veterans circling Trajan's column, the pivot of the poem's setting. The column is a product of history as well as a reminder of the cost of freedom. The 127-foot Roman Doric column of white marble contains 2,500 figures of soldiers, each two feet high. As landmark, moral guide, and time-nexus, the column in the poem is axis for the network of space-time vectors, of the past and present in a spiral pictorial narrative at once static and, as the couple circles, moving.

Hecht initially highlights the ignorance or indifference of the modern youths. When the soldiers are in focus, no reference is made to a past beyond their lives. When the modern youths are in focus, they are heedless of any historical responsibility. Both groups are immersed in their respective present; the difference is that the warriors change history whereas the young couple is oblivious to history.

Each group's consciousness or unconsciousness of history is articulated by the poem's two interjections. The noble, resonant voice of the past contrasts the shallow, shrill voice of the present. Midway in the poem, a voice intrudes to say the modern youths are unaware that their freedom was purchased at great cost.

This ancient voice "whispers inwardly, 'My soul, / It is the cost, the cost.'"
The idiomatic contemporary voice responds, "'Go screw yourself; all's fair in love
and war!'" The ante-penultimate stanza follows:

> Better they should not hear that whispered phrase,
>> The young Italian couple;
> Surely the mind in all its brave assays
>> Must put much thinking by,
> To be, as Yeats would have it, free and supple
>> As a long-legged fly.

The apparent directive is that the youths should remember the past and appreciate
the pain which purchased their freedom. After much contemplation of history, of
its significance to the present and ramifications for the future, they would become
in some sense liberated, as the first four stanzas show they already are. Like
athletes, if they stop to think, they are lost; reflecting on the past would cause them
to lose their equilibrium in the present:

> Look at their slender purchase, how they list
>> Like a blown clipper, brought
> To the lively edge of peril, to the kissed
>> Lip, the victor's crown,

> The prize of life. Yet one unbodied thought
>> Could topple them, bring down

> The whole shebang. . . .

Visual and auditory imagery further magnifies their thoughtlessness. The youth's girlfriend "grips the animal-shouldered naked skin / Of his fitted leather jacket"; his motorcycle's "flatulent racket" contrasts the slow, "solemn / Military pursuits" of the "scarred veterans coiling the stone."

Leaning the other way, the final stanza suggests it might be best, after all, for them to disregard the dubious success of the past.

> . . . And why should they take thought
>> Of all that ancient pain,
> The Danube winters, the nameless young who fought,
>> The blood's uncertain lease?
> Or remember that that fifteen-year campaign
>> Won seven years of peace?

The poem's epigraph, from *Hamlet* (III.ii.282-3), bears out this interpretation:

> *Why, let the stricken deer go weep,*
>> *The hart ungallèd play . . .*

The omitted couplet from Hamlet's mouth completes the meaning: "For some must watch while some must sleep, / Thus runs the world away" (III.ii.284-5).

Despite its equivocations, the poem seems finally to say that an informed freedom is better than a naive freedom heedless of its cost. The argument is dialectic: wars are fought for freedom; why then decry the youths' thoughtless freedom? Because they should remember the cost. But freedom-fighting should entail winning a present freedom free even from the *thought* of war, past or future. There should come a time when the past's pathologies are not allowed to taint present consciousness. And so on. Whatever the poem's moral stance towards historical consequences, the persona certainly envies the young couple's care-free innocence.

The shifting of foreground and background, the flipping of the coin's two faces of past and present, argues a synthesis, or median stance: one should neither dwell on nor ignore the past. The pitch of this enlightened voice would be a middle range between resonant and shrill. The emotional posture would fall between that of a "stricken deer" and a "hart ungallèd." The poem's rich diction, especially its proper names, also argues for a citizenry with manifold attitudes and for a time to every purpose under the heaven: "Vespa" (technology), "Trajan" (politics/war), "Calder" (art), "Dante" and "Yeats" (poetry), "Gregory the Great" (religion), "Lapith" (myth), "Othello" and his crew (love and intrigue). Surely the thoughtless Italian couple should enjoy their season.

Too, the "rival tugs" of line three prescribe a balance achieved through the tension of thought and action. The agile couple "Coasting the margins of those rival tugs / Down the thin path of friction" become emblematic of everything later mentioned that draws energy and direction from opposing forces: gulls, ships, athletes, Calder mobiles, Yeats' "long-legged fly." The first word of Hecht's poem, "Think," reminds us of that necessity in order "That civilisation may not sink," as Yeats' first line from "Long-legged Fly" warns.

The theme of "The Odds" is also expressed ambiguously. In a world of chance, adversity, and war, Hecht's third son, Evan Alexander, is born. His springtime birth would elicit optimism but for the fact that he might grow up merely to die in an absurd war, one whose dénouement will not bring even "seven years of peace." As in "The Cost," the background is war but this time an absurd war whose issue, to the American soldier at least, was not freedom.[5] The foreground again includes a love relationship.

The first four stanzas give the immediate background, a snowy landscape, a "stagy show / Put on by a spoiled, eccentric millionaire." In the fifth stanza, Hecht says the snowflakes are

> Like the blind, headlong cells,
> Crowding toward dreams of life, only to die
> In dark fallopian canals,
> Or that wild strew of bodies at My Lai.

The reader wonders what connection snowflakes have with sperm cells or what either has with the My Lai bodies. Hecht, an "eccentric millionaire" of words, patiently unfolds the full canvas in the next stanza to produce the foreground of the poem.

Yet to these April snows,

This rashness, those incalculable odds,

The costly and cold-blooded shows

Of blind perversity or spendthrift gods

My son is born, and in his mother's eyes

Turns the whole war and winter into lies.

The imagery gathers around the newborn: "unearthly wheat," "headlong cells," "bodies at My Lai." Will he be cultivated for war, and will he die needlessly? Whether the child's fate is dictated by "blind perversity" (deterministic factors) or by "spendthrift gods" (politicians and generals), "the odds" of his having a productive life are incalculable. To some, the war is more important than the boy's birth, but "in his mother's eyes" the devastation of "war and winter" is turned into a lie. Still, April remains the cruellest month.

But voices underground

Demand, "Who died for him? Who gave him place?"

I have no answer. Vaguely stunned,

I turn away and look at my wife's face.

Outside the simple miracle of this birth

The snowflakes lift and swivel to the earth

As in those crystal balls

> With Christmas storms of manageable size,
>
> . . . .
>
> A tiny settlement among those powers
>
> That shape our world, but that are never ours.

The father has "no answers" to the same questions posed in "The Cost": "'Who died for him? Who gave him place?'" He does not belittle the significance of the war, but his microcosm "of manageable size" takes precedence over it. In that world at least, he may cradle his son within his small circle of care and use his limited powers to shape his destiny.

A Crafty Transcendentalism

Characteristic of many of Hecht's poems is their similarity to the meditational exercises of the Puritans. In "Peripeteia," the object of meditation is a Shakespearean play, more specifically, the liminal moment before the curtain rises, when the viewer's consciousness is suspended between his isolation as a self and his involvement as a spectator. The poem, about Hecht's "finding and falling in love with [his] second wife,"[6] opens with the poet's observations as he waits for the lights to dim:

> . . . It is that stillness
>
> I wait for.

> Before it comes,
>
> Whether we like it or not, we are a crowd,
>
> Foul-breathed, gum-chewing, fat with arrogance,
>
> Passion, opinion, and appetite for blood.
>
> But in that instant, which the mind protracts,
>
> From dim to dark before the curtain rises,
>
> Each of us is miraculously alone
>
> . . . .
>
> As at the beginning and end, a single soul,
>
> With all the sweet and sour of loneliness.

The quiet moment of stasis points out the essential truth of the independent self, not realized in the flux of ordinary experience, which prevents introspection. The liminal experience causes a heightened awareness of the self as a perceiver of, and participant in, the world. Ironically, this calm comes before *The Tempest*, the play the speaker is about to see.

The speaker compares the dimness to an experience he had as a child, when he watched a similar obscurity take over the landscape before a storm. The persona says that such a comparison is

> A useful discipline, perhaps. One that might lead
>
> To solitary, self-denying work
>
> That issues in something harmless, like a poem,

> Governed by laws that stand for other laws,
>
> Both of which aim, through kindred disciplines,
>
> At the soul's knowledge and habiliment.

The "useful discipline," comparing liminal states, might lead to a poem. The discipline of contemplation and writing both are "governed by laws that stand for other laws" which, "through kindred disciplines," aim "at the soul's knowledge."

Hecht's use of the word "discipline" leads the reader to engage in a similar discipline of comparison, specifically, to compare Emerson's view of Nature as a discipline with the ideas Hecht expresses in "Peripeteia." The seminal statement of Chapter 6 of *Nature*, entitled "Discipline," reads, "Hence it is, that a rule of one art, or a law of one organization, holds true throughout nature."[7] The essay answers the question posed in its second paragraph: "Let us inquire, to what end is nature? . . . All the parts incessantly work into each other's hands for the profit of man."[8] Hecht says that the "kindred disciplines" lead, step by step, to "the soul's knowledge and habiliment," thus concurring with Emerson's belief that Nature is given as a ladder-like means to self-knowledge and to a true knowledge of the self's relation to the rest of the world.

The poem continues with another useful comparison. Just as Shakespeare compared the world to a stage, the speaker, who has called himself a "connoisseur of loneliness," compares the world to a dream.

> The play begins. Something by Shakespeare.
>
> Framed in the arched proscenium, it seems

A dream, neither better nor worse

Than whatever I shall dream after I rise

With hat and coat, go home to bed, and dream.

Predestined by their creator's words, the characters and actors "Perform their duties, even as I must mine, / Though not, as I am, always free to smile." But suddenly something peripeteiac (abrupt, unexpected) and dramatically impossible happens.

. . . As in a dream,

Leaving a stunned and gap-mouthed Ferdinand,

Father and faery pageant, she, even she,

Miraculous Miranda, steps from the stage,

Moves up the aisle to my seat, where she stops,

Smiles gently, seriously, and takes my hand

And leads me out of the theatre, into a night

As luminous as noon, more deeply real,

Simply because of her hand, than any dream

Shakespeare or I or anyone ever dreamed.

The poem's conclusion contains the Platonic notion that the world is Idea, or perhaps a dream in the mind of God; yet importantly, in Emersonian fashion, the poet does not disavow nature merely because he has discovered a higher reality. In fact, his new love pulls him out of the predestined arena into the "brave new world"

where they can write their own script. Like Milton's Adam and Eve, the world all
before them, hand in hand, the "connoisseur of loneliness" and his new companion
take their "solitary way."

In a later poem from *Millions of Strange Shadows*, "'Gladness of the Best,'" the
meditative objects are illuminated manuscripts and tapestries.[9] In viewing them,
the persona is reminded of the paradox of freedom and necessity and the fact that
various art forms of the seventeenth century reflect the same aesthetic principle.
From there, the poet is led to comment on the unity underlying diversity, a unity he
attributes, ultimately, to a benevolent and personal God.

In the first stanza, Hecht points out that in the Duc de Berry's *Très Riches Heures*
an untrellised vine entwines heaven and earth with the eyes of its beholder:

> See, see upon a field of royal blue,
> Scaling the steep escarpments of the sky
>   With gold-leafed curlicue,
> Sepals and plumula and filigree,
>   This vast, untrellised vine
> Of scroll- and fretwork, a Jesse's family tree
> Or ivy whose thick clamberings entwine
> Heaven and earth and the viewer's raddling eye.

In the second stanza, it becomes apparent that Hecht is imitating the florid style
of the illuminated manuscript and Gobelin tapestries in his diction and interweav-
ing rhymes:

This mealed and sprinkled glittering, this park

Of 'flowres delice' and Gobelin *millefleurs*

Coiling upon the dark

In wild tourbillions, gerbs and golden falls

Is a mere lace or grille

Before which Jesus works his miracles

Of love, feeding the poor, curing the ill,

Here in the Duc de Berry's *Très Riches Heures*;

This is the kind of exhibition that has caused some critics to label Hecht's style precious, yet the exotic words "tourbillions" and "*millefleurs*" fittingly describe the elegant manuscript and tapestries. Additionally, both stanzas are a complex interweave of syntax, rhyme (AB AC DC DB), and syllabic lines (10-10-6-10-6-10-10-10). The stanzas can be divided into halves of thirty-six syllables each (10-10-6-10 / 6-10-10-10) which form a counterpoint. Likewise, the rhyme scheme is in counterpoint: AB AC form a pattern in the first half, and D follows C to begin the next half; moreover, D_ D_ in the second half echoes A_ A_ in the first half, whereas _C _B in the second half is the mirror image of _B _C in the first half.

The next two stanzas suggest that all art forms are linked to one another by a common harmony:

And is itself the visible counterpart

Of fugal consort, branched polyphony,

That dense, embroidered art
Of interleaved and deftly braided song
In which each separate voice
Seems to discover where it should belong
Among its kind, and, fated by its choice,
Pursues a purpose at once fixed and free;

And every *cantus*, firm in its own pursuits,
Fluent and yet cast, as it were, in bronze,
Exchanges brief salutes
And bows of courtesy at every turn
With every neighboring friend,
Bends to oblige each one with quick concern
And join them at a predetermined end
Of cordial and confirming antiphons.

In song and vine, each "separate voice" pursues its own track and may diverge from the "neighboring friend" with which it began, but each voice or vine will rejoin (in the sense of "reconnect" *and* "reply to") its neighbor "at a predetermined end." The rhyme scheme verifies and completes this pattern, which remains to be demonstrated. Also, the statement that "each separate voice / Seems to discover where it should belong" contains the Aristotelian notion of *entelechy*, the idea that all things have a purpose or end for which they strive, a teleological and evolutionary view expressed by Emerson in the epigraph to *Nature* where he says that "the worm

/ Mounts through all the spires of form."

Several puns, some etymologically and some visually based, stitch together words within and between stanzas, thus reinforcing the theme of the interconnectedness of the world's objects and phenomena. The cantus firmus of fifteenth-century polyphony is recalled in the juxtaposed "*cantus*, firm" of the last stanza cited. The use of "fixed" in the line just before "*cantus*, firm" reminds the reader that "cantus firmus" is Medieval Latin for "fixed melody." Music and illuminated manuscript are termed "visible counterpart[s]." Fittingly, the music is expressed in terms of foliage and tapestry: "interleaved and deftly braided song." Less obviously, the separate voices of the "branched polyphony" are likened to stanza one's separate vines "whose thick clamberings entwine / Heaven and earth and the viewer's raddling eye": every "*cantus*," here in the context almost certainly punning on the acanthus leaf motif of Corinthian columns, diverges from its neighbor as if free to do so and yet converges finally with its neighbor as if fated to do so. Each leaf or voice acknowledges its antiphonal partner with "salutes" and "bows," bends to "oblige each one with quick concern." "Oblige" plays off of the musical term "obbligato," indicating something indispensable and not to be left out, yet in the context "oblige" means something done out of courtesy, not obligation, duty, or necessity. The root of "oblige," *ligare*, suggests a tying together, which is exactly the ligamental function of the visual and etymological puns here and throughout the poem. The placement of "oblige," which carries both meanings of favor and duty, between the words "courtesy" and "predetermined" tensely binds the contradictories here just as elsewhere in the poem antithetical or paradoxical elements are linked, notably free will and determinism in the phrases "fated by its choice" and "at once fixed and free." Tying the stanza currently under consideration to the next are the words "turn" and "join," which surface transformed or as self-conscious puns: "turn becomes the trope" and "enjoined."

The Gobelin tapestry, then, is a visible counterpart of the music of the century; "embroidered art" mirrors "deftly braided song." Yet the next stanza explains that tapestry and song, in turn, imitate and intimate the transcendent interlacing between God and man, "that holy amity which is our only hope." Christ, in whom Deity and humanity are spliced, links God and man. Furthermore, the poem has seven stanzas, an appropriate number in a poem about "holy amity," a phrase Hecht borrowed (and altered) from "Man," a poem by George Herbert, the St. George of stanza six. The last three stanzas of "'Gladness of the Best'":

Such music in its turn becomes the trope
Or figure of that holy amity
    Which is our only hope,
Enjoined upon us from two mountain heights:
    On Tables of The Law
Given at Sinai, and the Nazarite's
Luminous sermon that reduced to awe
And silence a vast crowd near Galilee.

Who could have known this better than St. George,
The Poet, in whose work these things are woven
    Or wrought as at a forge
Of disappointed hopes, of triumphs won

Through strains of sound and soul
In that small country church at Bemerton?
This was the man who styled his ghostly role,
"Domestic servant to the King of Heaven."

If then, as in the counterpoises of
Music, the laity may bless the priest
        In an exchange of love,
        Riposta for *Proposta*, all we inherit
            Returned and newly named
In the established words, "and with thy spirit,"
Be it with such clear grace as his who claimed,
Of all God's mercies, he was less than least.

In his editorial introduction to *The Essential Herbert*, Hecht cites the cleric's deathbed instructions that his poems be made public if they "may turn to the advantage of any dejected poor Soul" or be burned if not: "for I and it, are less than the least of God's mercies." Therein, Hecht also details "Herbert's fascination with music."[10]

The rhyme scheme of the poem is circular and complete, beginning with A and ending with Z, and imitates God's holy amity, the illuminated manuscript, the music, and the tapestry—in short, the entire harmonious universe. Plotted out, the rhyme scheme is: A B A C D C D B // E F E G H G H F // I C I J K J K C // L M L N O N O M // P C P Q R Q R C // S T S U V U V T // W X W Y Z Y Z X. The poem does not end in Z because, polyphonically, the penultimate rhyme of each stanza determines (alphabetically) the initial rhyme of the succeeding stanza. Thus, D in the penultimate position of stanza one is followed by E in the initial position of stanza two and so on until the penultimate rhyme of stanza seven (Z) must return to the initial rhyme of stanza one (A) in a circular question-answer or *"Riposta* for *Proposta"* fashion, as the speaker says in the last stanza. The pattern recognizable (after some frowning) in the alphabetic notation is virtually undetectable in the sequence of rhyming sounds themselves. Perhaps the alphabetic notation is analogous to conventional musical notation. In any case, only an extreme fortuity (to which I am not willing to subscribe) could account for such an involved symmetry.

The poem argues that the unity of various art forms reflects a unifying transcendent harmony. As Emerson said:

Thus architecture is called "frozen music," by De Stael and Goethe. Vitrivius thought an architect should be a musician. "A Gothic church," said Coleridge, "is a petrified religion." Michael Angelo maintained, that, to an architect, a knowledge of anatomy is essential. In Haydn's oratorios, the notes present to the imagination not only motions, as, of the snake, the stag, and the elephant, but colors also; as the green grass. The law of harmonic sounds reappears in the harmonic colors. . . . Hence it is, that a rule of one art, or a law of one organization, holds true throughout nature. So intimate is this Unity, that, it is

easily seen, it lies under the undermost garment of nature, and
betrays its source in universal Spirit. For, it pervades Thought
also. Every universal truth which we express in words, implies
or supposes every other truth. . . . Every such truth is the absolute Ens seen from one side. But it has innumerable sides.[11]

In Hecht's work, transcendental themes are intimated as early as "A Poem for Julia"
in *A Summoning of Stones* (1954). In *Millions of Strange Shadows* (1977), Hecht
returns to the theme in five poems besides "'Gladness of the Best.'" In "Green: An
Epistle," for instance, landscapes and nature's growth processes symbolize for
Hecht, as they did for Emerson, "a code / Or muffled intimation / Of purposes and
preordained events" (from "Still Life," *The Venetian Vespers*). The other poems
from *Shadows* are "Swan Dive," "'Dichtung und Wahrheit,'" "Apprehensions,"
and "The Lull," which ends the volume with a more direct transcendental statement
than is found in the previously mentioned poems.

The Liminal Poems

In *Shadows*, Hecht introduces a new theme in poems that may justly be called
epistemological vignettes, poems that treat liminal experiences, akin to Wordsworth's
"spots of time," as psychological phenomena which tell us something about the
nature of reality. As its root, limen, implies, an experience or place is liminal if it
is on a threshold: twilight or dawn (neither day nor night), a window (neither in- nor

outside), or a transitional state of mind like intuition or near-sleep (neither conscious nor unconscious). Though seemingly unimportant at the time, the experiences are like Wordsworth's "spots" in their vividness and tenacious hold on the memory.

In "Swan Dive," Hecht uses a liminal moment, the apex of a dive, to make metaphysical assertions. It begins as celebration of an aesthetic athleticism. By poem's end, the title carries weightier echoes of swan song and the Fall of Man.

Stanza one exhibits what might be called "pure Hecht," description of the poem's exterior setting, which in the refractions of light and water represents the flux or confusion of the world:

> Over a crisp regatta of lights, or a school
> Of bobbling spoons, ovals of polished black
> Kiss, link, and part, wriggle and ride in place
> On the lilt and rippling slide of the waterback,
> And glints go skittering in a down-wind race
> On smooth librations of the swimming pool,

the next stanza delineating the interior setting:

> While overhead on the tensile jut and spring
> Of the highest board, a saffroned diver toes

The sisal edge, rehearsing throughout his limbs
The flight of himself, from the arching glee to the close
Of wet, complete acceptance. . . .

The next four stanzas recount the dive itself, performed before, but not for, voyeuristic nonparticipants: "the foreshortened girls and boys / Below in a world of envies and desires." Emphasized is the solipsistic engagement of the diver, symbol of any artist. In a description rife with Platonic overtones, he rehearses, before the dive, "The flight of himself, from the arching glee to the close," after which he rises, in actuality, to a "Realm of his own, a destined place in the air," his mental rehearsal now realized, or, more Platonically, the Idea of the dive now reified.

"His dream of himself requires," among other things, a "sleek Daedalian poise," suggesting the difference between disciplined thought and high-flying fancy dramatized in the contrasting fates of Daedalus and Icarus. From this evanescently perfect stasis at the dive's zenith, fairly interpreted either as a tiny death or an intimation of immortality, "he bows his head with abrupt assent / And sails to a perfect sacrifice below," again resident in the "world of envies and desires." Bowing "his head with abrupt assent" implies servile but reluctant obedience to physical laws, the pun on assent/ascent highlighting the tension between wish and reality.

The bowing head, sacrifice, and fall into water, a "Tumult of haloes in green, cathedral light"—all emphasize the religious aspect of his dive. He was weightless in air, is now bouyant in water, and his performance would be successful but for the fact that from the ideal form of the dive he falls into a world of corrupted substance, as the initial lines of the final stanza show: "But hoisting himself out, his weight returns / To normal, like sudden aging or weariness." At the dive's apex, he escapes the limitations of his body; emerging from the water, he dons his sloughed-off body.

The remaining lines disclose another brand of rehearsal and ritual sacrifice in the world of desires.

> Tonight, full-length on a rumpled bed, alone,
> He will redream it all: bathed in success
> And sweat, he will achieve the chiselled stone
> Of catatonia, for which his body yearns.

Because of the autoerotic terms, the last stanza, and perhaps the entire poem, begs to be read as sexual metaphor: on the high board, the diver imagines the whole process, from "arching glee to the close / Of wet, complete acceptance," from which he surfaces "into a final calm ... / Where he rides limp and smilingly at ease." After his artistic act, he is "limp"; the night-fantasy results in "stone"—and not the stone of erection, but "the chiselled stone / Of catatonia," that is, the sleep of postorgasmic narcosis. Both dreams end in the "complete acceptance" of line 11, a freedom from trying. Thus, sexual release and contemplation of the Ideal free us from the world of the body and its demands, if only until it recharges.

The poem concludes with "yearns," a word implying a frustration endemic to the world of the body. In this sense, "Swan Dive" is related to the Sisyphus myth and Frost's "Birches," with the difference that, in his contest, Hecht's protagonist desires stasis, not a dialectical swinging from earth to heaven and back. In sleep, as at the pinnacle of the dive, the man can (and, importantly, wants to) forget the limitations of his body, or even that he has a body. His is not a lover's quarrel with the world.

The poem is a variation on Hecht's painting-as-permanence motif. The dive partakes of the "metastasis of art," as "The Venetian Vespers" puts it, "our happiest, most cherished dream / Of paradise": "arrested action, an escape / From time . . . / Into the blessèd stasis of a painting." The achievement of "Swan Dive" lies in its honesty about the facts of this world, felt in the frustration of the poem's last lines, where the diver's act can attain the stasis of plastic art no more than a person can levitate or achieve suspended animation. The diver's mobile art must be repeated to be appreciated anew.

Dive and autoerotism point to the desire for transcendence. Both consummations, in their ecstasy followed by quiescence, are equated with perfect death: blissful, fulfilling, and, best of all, repeatable—solo flights from which and, significantly, to which one can return. Thus, the symbolic dive is paradoxical in that it is both a death dive ("swan" dive) and death-defying.

Ultimately, dive and sex as poetic analogies for perfect death (the diver can climb the board again, the onanist can revive his erection) fail because they cannot symbolize what the poem's diver wants—stoppage from the vacillating nature of the world of his body. The poem realizes this and ends in a momentary stay, though with ultimate frustration embedded in the dramatic situation—the protagonist will reawaken to his Sisyphean task. Here is no boyish glee at the metronomic oscillation of mental states, no old man's relishing of fluctuating ontology, and no desire for compromise. This protagonist desires either perfect aesthetic poise or perfectly anesthetic catatonia.

It might not be going too far to say that "stone" and "shadow" here symbolize the One and the Many of pre-Socratic philosophy. In "Swan Dive," as in many poems from *Stones* to *Hours*, the One and the Many (or stasis and flux) are symbolized in "stone" and "shadows." "Shadow" or its variants show up in nearly every poem from *Stones* to *Shadows*. The motif can be traced through several liminal poems to the last poem of *Shadows*, "The Lull," in which the world emerges shadowless.

In "Peripeteia," a fallen world (implicit in the Platonic allusions) and salvation (through love experienced in that world) from it to a higher reality are dramatized. "'Dichtung und Wahrheit,'" the title of Goethe's autobiography, also contains Platonic and Shakespearean analogues which suggest a fallen world and a formula (in this case, poetry) for renewing the world. The meditative objects in "Dichtung" are a piece of sculpture and a photograph, static objects that, like the snapshot in "A Birthday Poem," stop time, motion, and aging. Poems already discussed in other contexts, but which also have arrested action as controlling images, include "The Cost," "A Birthday Poem," "Swan Dive," and "Peripeteia." "Dichtung," "Apprehensions," "After the Rain," and "The Lull" reveal explicitly the metaphysical problems or epistemological conclusions which in the other poems are undeveloped or implicit.

In "'Dichtung und Wahrheit,'" Hecht returns to the formula of his earlier meditative poems: presenting a static object and documenting the persona's thoughts as they unreel before the object. Here, the artifacts are idealized copies of changeful reality:

> The Discus Thrower's marble heave,
>
> Captured in mid-career,
>
> . . . .
>
> This, and the clumsy snapshot of
>
> An infantry platoon,
>
> . . . .
>
> Stop history in its tracks.

The references in stanza one to Vesalius, sixteenth-century father of anatomy, and in stanza two to taxidermy broach the poem's eventual topic, spiritual anatomy and the world as key to liberating the secrets locked in the "granite prisons / And oubliettes of the soul." The second stanza explores the significance of the history-stopping artifacts of stanza one.

> We who are all aswim in time,
>
> We, "the inconstant ones,"
>
> How can such fixture speak to us?

This single question generates others. How can stasis reveal something about reality that its normal fluxionary manifestation cannot? Does that mutable reality, in turn, borrow its essence from a still "more real" reality? If so, can that reality be forced to yield deeper meanings? No new tune here, it's the old Platonic shuffle.

That art arrests us in life-like postures is obliquely and, according to one's tastes, humorously or gruesomely alluded to in the reference to Jeremy Bentham, who, by his last will and testament, had himself stuffed.

> The chisel and the lens
> Deal in a taxidermy
> Of our arrested flights,
> And by their brute translation we
> Turn into Benthamites.

Bentham died on June 6, 1832, in his eighty-fifth year. Following his instructions, his body was dissected in the presence of his friends. His skeleton was reconstructed and supplied with a wax head to replace the original, which had been mummified. The effigy, dressed in his own clothes and set upright in a glass case, can be seen to this day in University College, London, in his dated attire, his stovepipe hat on the floor beside him.

In Part II of the poem, the persona observes that all art partakes of a transcendent harmony:

> Easy enough to claim, in the dawn of hindsight,
> That Mozart's music perfectly enacts
> Pastries and powdered wigs, an architecture

Of white and gold rosettes, balanced parterres.

More difficult to know how the spirit learns

Its scales, or the exact dimensions of fear:

The nameless man dressed head-to-foot in black,

Come to commission a requiem in a hurry.

The "nameless man" is the mysterious stranger, magnified to a death messenger by Mozart's overwrought imagination, who ordered the *Requiem* for an undisclosed patron. This nameless stranger, theatrically bedecked in symbolic costume, was perhaps apocryphally identified as Salieri in Peter Shaffer's 1980 play and 1984 film *Amadeus*.

. . . Just how such [spiritual] truth

Gets itself stated in pralltrillers and mordents

Not everyone can say. . . .

"Such truth," that there is a single unifying principle mysteriously informing an apparently diverse world, is a manifestly Platonic notion. Again, Emerson's expression of transcendent harmony applies: "Hence it is, that a rule of one art, or a law of one organization, holds true throughout nature."[12]

The second stanza of Part II contains three statements about three important realities: the Word, the world, and "texts," replicas of things in the world. The stanza opens,

> We begin [at birth] with the supreme donnée, the world,
>
> Upon which every text is commentary,
>
> And yet they [world and text] play each other. . . .

From birth, we attempt to understand the world through static "texts" such as books, sculpture, painting, photography, architecture, even music and mathematics—whose static notations represent fluid realities. This cross-energetic mimesis extends even to ridiculous counterparts such as "pastries and powdered wigs" and, in *Stones*, the formal gardens of "La Condition Botanique" and "The Gardens of the Villa d'Este." There are two facets of the first major statement: that the world determines texts and that texts reflect (and alter) the world. Compare Wallace Stevens' similar statements: "Life consists / Of propositions about life" ("Men Made out of Words") and "there never was a world for her / Except the one she sang and, singing, made" ("The Idea of Order at Key West").

The second major statement—that the perceiver, not the world, needs to be renewed—occurs in the middle of the stanza.

> It is, in the end, the solitary scholar
>
> Who returns us to the freshness of the text,
>
> Which returns to us the freshness of the world
>
> In which we find ourselves, like replicas,
>
> Dazzled by glittering dawns, upon a stage.

Because texts sometimes mislead us and errantly determine our view of the world, we need the solitary scholar (critic, metaphysician, poet, any artist) to return "*us* to the freshness of the text." The text is accurate and does not need refreshing. In turn, the freshness of the text "returns *to us* the freshness of the world." Because our adult concepts prejudice our percepts, the scholar must, insofar as possible, return us to original perception. Rid of at least some *a priori* ideas, we can again see the world with the pristine vision of a child. Our eyes, dulled by the world's manifold impressions, are renewed when we see an object of nature isolated as an artifact of beauty which partakes of the universal Beauty of nature. Thereafter, we see the Unity in nature and see ourselves as replicas (such as those in Plato's Allegory of the Cave) on a stage.

The third major statement—that mediating words clarify both texts and world—is found in the poem's final line:

> Enter the Prologue, who at once declares,
> "We begin with the supreme donnée, the word."

The supreme, primordial given is not, after all, the world, but the word. Or rather they have co-primacy of importance; word and text "play each other," as the poem earlier states. The reason for the poem's being dedicated to Cyrus Hoy, professor of Renaissance drama at the University of Rochester, becomes apparent in the last stanza's vignette with its mystical Prologue who is likened to an Elizabethan prologue such as that in *Henry V*. Here, the prologue is the rising sun, but by extension light or Light, God, the creative principle, Logos, the Son. The replicas find their origin in this Logos. Genesis 1 records God speaking the world into being. John 1 presents the equation: Word/Logos=God=Life=Light=Christ.

The poem's central theme is that the world and texts mutually affect each other. Were world and texts the only realities, the question "How can such fixture speak to us?" would have to be answered, "Such fixture cannot speak to us." But, because the Scholar returns us to the text, which returns us to the world, which returns us to the primary reality, the Word, the question can be answered, "Such fixture speaks to us by pointing to progressively higher realities until we reach transcendent reality, from which we receive our being and derive our meaning." The poet is the Emersonian god-man who, through art, can give us back the wonders of the world and ourselves. "Dichtung und Wahrheit," whether translated "fiction and reality" or "poetry and truth" indicates that fictions (representational codes such as photographs and sculpture) and poetry (words) reveal fragments of ultimate reality or truth. Poetry and truth are intimately related, whereas the popular assumption is that they are the opposite of one another. Wallace Stevens takes his magnificent gibes at the popular notion in "A High-Toned Old Christian Woman": "Poetry is the supreme fiction, madame. . . . But fictive things / Wink as they will. Wink most when widows wince."

Hecht's obsession with stasis in *Shadows* suggests a movement towards a final philosophical answer to the question nagging him since "A Poem for Julia," from *Stones*: "But in our fallen state . . . / What do we know of lasting since the fall?" The makeshift answer had been either "nothing" or that, since the fall, what we know of lasting is found in the stasis of art. In *Shadows*, stasis points to a higher reality, the permanent One. The concern with stasis from *Stones* to *Shadows* presumes a fall, cosmological, moral, or perceptual. Hecht's poetry is concerned mainly with the fall from true perception. It is that primary perception of the world, recorded in the Wordsworthian childhood of "Apprehensions," that makes Hecht, at least as the persona he presents in his poems, aware of the need for a renewal of perception. As if following Ransom's lead, Hecht achieves this renewal through poetry. In his influential essay "Wanted: An Ontological Critic," Ransom said, "Poetry intends to recover the denser and more refractory original world which we know loosely through our perceptions and memories. By this supposition it is a kind of knowledge which is radically or ontologically distinct."[13] In "Apprehensions," the persona recalls his last "distinct and legible" vision of the world:

> And all of this made me superbly happy,
> But most of all a yellow Checker Cab
> Parked at the corner. Something in the light
> Was making this the yellowest thing on earth.
> It was as if Adam, having completed
> Naming the animals, had started in
> On colors, and had found his primary pigment
> Here, in a taxi cab, on Eighty-ninth street.
> It was the absolute, parental yellow.

The death of the distinctive childhood vision is signaled by the closing of a window: "Someone or other / Called me away from there, and closed the window." How to return to the childhood side of the window of perception is a major concern of *Millions of Strange Shadows*.

By the time *Shadows* was published, twelve years after *Hours*, Hecht was more consciously on the trail of the lost perception of childhood than when "A Hill," which records a "spot of time" from childhood, was written. "After the Rain" and "The Lull" complete the movement of *Shadows* and conclude the metaphysical quest chronicled in *Stones*, *Hours*, and *Shadows*. Significantly, the two poems record liminal experiences just before and after storms like that in "Apprehensions" which marked the boy's last unclouded vision of the world.

"After the Rain" portrays its speaker not as detached observer of nature but as a man whose moods correspond to nature's landscapes as if he were Emerson himself. During the lull after a night of rain, "some early, innocent lust" matching nature's gets him outdoors "to smell / The teasle, the pelted bracken, / The cold, mossed-over well. . . ." The rain droplets have run together in serpentine forms "as though pledged / To attain a difficult goal / And join some important river."

The landscape resembles the pristine and, as in "A Hill," sometimes barren landscapes he saw as a child. Like other liminal poems in which the innocent perception is momentarily recovered, this poem contains scenery static and shadowless:

> How even and pure this light!
> All things stand on their own,
> Equal and shadowless,
> In a world gone pale and neuter,

> Yet riddled with fresh delight.
> The heart of every stone
> Conceals a toad, and the grass
> Shines with a douse of pewter.

Several things are remarkable about this stretch of text. First, the words and images resemble those used to convey the vision in "Apprehensions." The silence, the pure and even light, the fact that "All things stand on their own, / Equal and shadowless," and the "fresh delight" of the world mirror passages from "Apprehensions": "the air . . . stood still," the "luminous" streets, "everything / Seemed meant to be as it was, seemed so designed," and the "uncanny freshness" of the world.

Second, the line "the heart of every stone / Conceals a toad" resembles the Pythagorean, Platonic, animistic, and transcendental notions that every object has a soul or spirit. The line seems to be a reversal of *As You Like It* (II.i.11-13): "Sweet are the uses of adversity, / Which, like the toad, ugly and venomous, / Wears yet a precious jewel in his head."

For all this renewal of perception, the speaker is only momentarily immersed in nature. He starts from his intuitive reverie and "thinks" of nature's signs. This returns him to the posture of empirical observer and returns nature to the category of object. Still, his impressive experience makes his words echo "the Spartan fairness" he has seen:

> This queer, delicious bareness,
> This plain, uniform light,

In which both elms and thistles,

Grass, boulders, even words,

Speak for a Spartan fairness,

Might, as I think it over,

Speak in a form of signs,

If only one could know

All of its hidden tricks,

Saying that I must go

With a cool taste of coins

To join some important river,

Some damp and swollen Styx.

Hard, bare words convey hard, bare images and thoughts. In the passage, fifty-one of the sixty-six words are monosyllabic. Even among the polysyllables, there are no grandiloquent words such as the "tourbillions," "*millefleurs*," "plumula and filigree" found in "'Gladness of the Best.'" Instead, the diction corresponds, one word to one thing, to the discreteness of nature's objects.

The speaker finds nature's moods contagious. Just as the droplets forming a stream must eventually run into a larger body of water, he sees that he too *might* go "To join some important river," but, though he notes the analogy, he cannot be certain of its truth because he cannot decipher nature's hieroglyphs: "This plain, uniform light . . . // Might . . . / Speak in a form of signs, / If only one could know

/ All of its hidden tricks."[14] This idea continues the tradition of "nature speaking" running through the pre-Socratics, Puritans, and transcendentalists. The morality that may be embedded in nature is embedded, sometimes cleverly, in the poem's diction: "uprights," "innocent," "even and pure," "equal," "right," "fairness," "pure and just."

Hecht notes in his essay "The Pathetic Fallacy," from *Obbligati*, that "The world as holy cipher and mute articulator can be found not only in medieval texts and Shakespeare but in those emblematic or symbolic poems by Herbert and Donne and Herrick that are among the great achievements of their age. . . ."[15] Earlier in the same essay, Hecht says that the "emblematic mode of viewing nature" is

> . . . premised on the conviction that the whole purpose and
> majesty of God is made legible in the most minute, as well as
> the most stunning and conspicuous, parts of his creation; that
> attentive contemplation of any single part will reveal *in code*
> *but with clarity* the whole glory and intent of the Creator.[16]

This notwithstanding, the speaker of "After the Rain" doubts his experience, despite having viewed unveiled nature through the "open window" of perception.

> Yet what puzzles me most
> Is my unwavering taste
> For these dim, weathery ghosts,
> And how, from the very first,

An early, innocent lust
Delighted in such wastes,
Sought with a reckless thirst
A light so pure and just.

This final stanza contradicts the experience of the previous six, and the speaker protests too much when he calls the landscapes "wastes." As the bleak vision in "A Hill" attests, "from the very first," from childhood, the only time when lust is innocent, he has been attracted to the aesthetics of stark landscapes, and has "Delighted in such wastes."

"The Lull," the last poem of *Shadows*, also is tinctured with transcendental overtones. The setting and events parallel those in "After the Rain," though here the speaker does not doubt his experience and the lull comes *before* a rain. In "Apprehensions," the window of the boy's perception was closed in a lull before a storm: "Someone or other / Called me away from there, and closed the window." Now, after many years, that window is re-opened.

The first three stanzas paint a scene of trees waving in the breeze and casting lambent shadows over the lawn, water, and "tiled and tessellated floor." As in the lull before the storm of "Apprehensions," where suddenly "the air, / Full of excited imminence, stood still," the air in "The Lull" abruptly stills:

. . . just now the air
Came to a sudden hush, and everywhere

> Things harden to an etched
> And iron immobility. . . .

This static moment also finds counterpart in "After the Rain." The fourth and fifth stanzas point out the liminal nature of the lull and call to mind the waiting "connoisseur of loneliness" in "Peripeteia."

> Instinctively the mind withdraws
> To airports, depots, the long, plotless pause
>
> Between the acts of a play,
> Those neuter, intermediary states
> Of vacancy and tedium and delay
> When it must wait and wait, as now it waits
> For a Wagnerian storm to roll
> Thunder along the streets and drench the soul.

The next stanzas duplicate the mood and description of both "Apprehensions" and "After the Rain."

> Meanwhile, the trustful eye,
> Content to notice merely what is there,

Remarks the ghostly phosphors of the sky,

The cast of mercury vapor everywhere—

Some shadowless, unfocussed light

In which all things come into their own right,

Pebble and weed and leaf

Distinct, refreshed, and cleanly self-defined,

Rapt in a trance of stillness, in a brief

Mood of serenity, as if designed

To be here now, and manifest

The deep, unvexed composure of the blessed.

This "shadowless, unfocussed light / In which all things come into their own right / . . . self-defined" finds analogues in the "luminous" light created by refractions off cloud bottoms in "Apprehensions" and in the things that "stand on their own, / Equal and shadowless" in "After the Rain."

Similarly, the phrase "Pebble . . . / Distinct, refreshed" matches imagery in "Apprehensions" ("the world / Glinted and shone with an uncanny *freshness*. . . . / Became *distinct* and legible") and in "After the Rain" ("All things stand on their own / Equal and shadowless . . . / Yet riddled with *fresh* delight. / The heart of every *stone* / Conceals a toad") [italics added].

Each object in "The Lull" possesses "a brief / Mood of serenity, as if designed / To be here now." This finds semantic counterpart in "Apprehensions" where "everything / Seemed meant to be as it was, seemed so designed" and a dramatized counterpart in "After the Rain": "Somewhere a branch rustles / With the life of squirrels or birds, / Some life that is quick and right."

The particularity of things, one of the marks of an unfallen perception, is revived in the second to last stanza:

> The seamed, impastoed bark,
> The cool, imperial certainty of stone,
> Antique leaf-lace, all these are bathed in a dark
> Mushroom and mineral odor of their own,
> Their inwardness made clear and sure
> As voice and fingerprint and signature.

To the child's visual paradise regained, the poet adds perception of the objects' "inwardness," epitomized in "The heart of every stone / Conceals a toad" from "After the Rain." Ransom says that "ideas have extension and objects have intension, but extension is thin while intension is thick."[17] Each object carries a message in the "voice and fingerprint and signature" of God. According to Emerson,

> By degrees we may come to know the primitive sense of the permanent objects of nature, so that the world shall be to us an open book, and every form significant of its hidden life and final cause.[18]

Emerson's "final cause" (what caused its existence, but also, in Aristotelian thought, its purpose or "end") is the transcendental reality which Hecht's persona discovers as informing the world. Emerson's "hidden life" is Hecht's "toad" and Whitman's "grass" that the good gray poet calls "the handkerchief of the Lord, / . . . designedly dropt, / Bearing the owner's name someway in the corners. . . ." The etymology of Emerson's "*sign*ificant," Whitman's "de*sign*edly," and Hecht's "*sign*ature" implies in each case God's veiled "sign" or coded mark of His presence.

The concluding stanza of *Millions of Strange Shadows*:

> The rain, of course, will come
> With grandstand flourishes and hullabaloo,
> The silvered streets, flashbulb and kettledrum,
> To douse and rouse the citizens, to strew
> Its rhinestones randomly, piecemeal.
> But for the moment the whole world is real.

The final short sentence stands emphatically isolated from its showy predecessor. Here, the major motifs of Hecht's first three volumes converge: the dead stones of the first volume come alive, the hard hours have passed, the shadows disappear, and the world is renewed with reclaimed vision—as the last phrase of *Shadows* celebrates, "the whole world is real."

The almost too felicitous conclusion is latent in the epigraph of volume one: ". . . to call the stones themselves to their ideal places, and enchant the very substance and skeleton of the world" (Santayana). The third book's title alludes to Shakespeare's lines: "What is your substance, whereof are you made, / That millions of strange shadows on you tend?" The substance whereof we are made is stones—not the lifeless stones of the first book, but enchanted stones.

Hecht's role in *Millions of Strange Shadows* is that of the "solitary scholar" of "'Dichtung und Wahrheit'" who "returns us to the freshness of the text, / Which returns to us the freshness of the world." The poet's role is reiterated in "A Lot of Night Music," wherein the bird whistling a "light vestigial / Reminder of a time, / An Aesopic Age when all the beasts were moral / And taught their ways to men" is the poet reporting glimpses of lost vision, recovered in liminal moments. "Night Music" appoints the firefly-poet as the "solitary scholar" to recover for us, through his "own lights" in a dark time, the lost innocence of vision. The poem's close optimistically states that even "Apollo's laurel / Blooms in [this] world made innocent again."

The Lighter Side

"The Ghost in the Martini" does not fall under any convenient rubric, yet it is such an intriguing poem that by default I serve it up as an addendum to this chapter. The poem dramatizes a conflict of conscience experienced by an older speaker as he "consider[s] a pass" on a young woman at a party. Unlike the *deus ex machina* of classical drama, used to resolve hopelessly tangled plots, Hecht's ghost from the martini humorously creates problems. The martini releases the animal instincts of the id, and, as the speaker muses "on the salt and battery / of the sexual clinch," the ego, come to the rescue, emerges from the drink as the disembodied voice of a young man. After some choice words ("You lousy son-of-a-bitch! // . . . You arrogant, elderly letch, you broken down / Brother of Apeneck Sweeney!"), the voice subsides and the speaker grabs the girl's arm to escape before the voice "opens his trap again."

Part of the poem's value lies in Hecht's clever modernizing of the medieval Body and Soul debate lyrics. Instead of an ontological duality, man, now a metaphorical triad, is divided into warring animal and social selves, the id and super-ego, with the ego as arbiter in the endless conflict. This metaphor finds expression in other contemporary poems, such as Tom Wayman's "Wayman in Love," in which Freudian and Marxist ideas, reified as the bearded sages them-selves, "climb in under the covers" where a young couple who only "want . . . to be left alone" are trying spontaneously to couple. Wayman's poem concludes with Freud's diagnosis: "'I can see . . . / that you two have problems,'" their immediate logistical problem being the intrusion of personified exterior social restrictions. Itself quasi-Marxist, "The Ghost in the Martini" speaks of the sexual transaction in economic terms: "wages / Of sin," "union scale," "Strike." The persona, in his Prufrockian inability to put a whole woman together, divides the girl into parts like a side of beef: "bosom," "lips," "eyes," "elbow," "ear."

What differentiates Hecht's poem from and elevates it above others of its ilk is its harder philosophical basis, albeit laced with ironic good humor.[19] Tucked neatly away in the punning title is the creeping skepticism of a rational age. "The Ghost in the Martini" alludes to "the Ghost in the Machine," Gilbert Ryle's tag for Descartes' perpetuation of the long-standing dogma that humans are divided into minds and bodies of different substances. The problem, of course, is one of

Tinkertoys: how can two truly different substances interact? The long and the short of Ryle's argument is that he wishes to evict the Ghost-mind from the Machine-body, the how and the where of the mind-body nexus incapable of being resolved. Given Ryle's stance ("Absolute solitude is . . . the ineluctable destiny of the soul. Only our bodies can meet."), it is no wonder the *senex amans* in Hecht's poem chooses to ignore the irritating Ghost and, telling the young woman "to find her purse," to opt for the bodily connection.[20]

CHAPTER FOUR
The Venetian Vespers

Old Pain, New Patterns

Published only two years after *Millions of Strange Shadows*, *The Venetian Vespers* contains poems signaling new directions alongside poems recycling the techniques refined in Hecht's first three volumes. In the long poems "The Venetian Vespers" and "The Short End," Hecht assays the strengths of the interior monologue and long narrative poem in the hands of an essentially lyric poet. The wholly fabricated characters bear no resemblance to the authorial presence, thinly disguised, in many of the early poems.

The middle poems of *Vespers* include earlier concerns, pains which, if we take the dedication at face value, no longer exist:

For HELEN

Whatever pain is figured in these pages,
Whatever voice here grieves,
Belonged to other lives and distant ages
Mnemosyne retrieves;
But all the joys and forces of invention
That can transmute to true
Gold these base matters floated in suspension
Are due alone to you.

"Persistences" is one of the poems in which old pain lingers. The poem follows the pattern of presenting a background and then a closing foreground whose meaning is enhanced by the background. The speaker resolves to be a mouthpiece for the "burning, voiceless Jews" who, "numberless as flakes," dreamlike, "press in dense approaches" as if to petition him. In a 1984 interview, Hecht recounted his emotions upon discovering mass graves near Buchenwald: "What I experienced in the war was not anywhere near so terrible as having been a prisoner in one of those camps, or having died or lost a family in one. So even I am considerably distanced from the calamities that happened to so many there. Yet my sense of it is much more alive than that of the average American citizen, and I feel somehow under an obligation to not let anyone forget how terrible that was."[1]

In "Persistences" as in the other backward-looking poems from *Vespers*, outer weather forecasts inner. "The leafless trees are feathery, / . . . / Blank, washed-out, commonplace." "The obscurity resembles" not the Flemish staggered planes the third book enlisted for thematic duty but "silken Chinese mist / Wherein through calligraphic daubs / Of artistry persist" the "Shingled and burnished armor-plate / Of sacred, child-eyed carp." This gauzy world of carp worship contrasts the stark world in which humans are less valued than fish, in which human anti-worship manifests itself in pogroms and internecine war.

Such is the world of "The Deodand," in which by a curious application of "justice" a young French Legionnaire is made to pay most cruelly for the "spiritual debauch" of a bevy of French women who mime a harem's dominance-submission roles—a "strange charade" for which "Exactions shall be made, an expiation, / A forfeiture." As the persona relates in a pedestrian manner, "Those who will not be taught by history / Have as their curse the office to repeat it. . . ." Captured by the

Algerians, the young Legionnaire is whorishly dressed as "La Belle France" and, after his fingers are amputated, is taken from "Encampment to encampment, on a leash, / And forced to beg for his food with a special verse / Sung to a popular show tune of those days."

Describing it as "a meditation on a Renoir painting entitled *Parisians Dressed in Algerian Costume*" (Hecht identifies the painting in a note), Brad Leithauser calls the poem "perhaps the most harrowing that Hecht has written," "a complex deliberation on the intertwined fates of innocence and evil. What these women are guilty of is an inattentiveness to the past—a failure to perceive the networks of complicity and cruelty that pervade their lives."[2]

"Still Life" sneaks up on its reader like an enemy. The poem pretends to present an idyllic landscape, perhaps in the Constable or Gainsborough vein:

> Sleep-walking vapor, like a visitant ghost,
>   Hovers above a lake
> Of Tennysonian calm just before dawn.
> Inverted trees and boulders waver and coast
> In polished darkness. Glints of silver break
> Among the liquid leafage, and then are gone.

The vision seems to be drifting to a pastoral close when, through prepositions, it zeroes in on the persona,

> I stand beneath a pine-tree in the cold,
>
> Just before dawn, somewhere in Germany,
>
> A cold, wet, Garand rifle in my hands,

and causes the reader to backtrack and reshuffle the poem's images in the context of war: another meaning of "Still Life" is death.

The poem is more a rephrasing than a renovating of the Emersonian correspondence theme successfully employed in the first three volumes:

> Why does this so much stir me, like a code
>
> Or muffled intimation
>
> Of purposes and preordained events?
>
> It knows me, and I recognize its mode. . . .

"Auspices" has the same effect. Although the current meaning of "auspices" implies being under a patron's favor, "Auspices," via its etymology, forebodes ill: avis plus *specere*, divination of the future by looking at birds. After the title's exhumation of its ancestral meaning, old structures and themes are invoked: "These are the wilds / Of loneliness, huge, vacant, sour and plain"; "The fearfullest desolations of the soul / Image themselves as local and abiding." Many of Hecht's poems, going back at least to "A Hill," dramatize this notion more forcefully than it is stated here, and "baneberry" and "beggarweeds" seem too self-consciously metaphoric. Far from being unsuccessful, these poems and their quiet strength evince a sure, shaping hand, yet they come off a mite stale if one reads Hecht in large chronological doses.

The longer poems of *Vespers* have the feel of a poet turning to fresher tasks in the nick of time, and the new direction of the title poem by no means gives the effect of a man testing chill waters with reluctant toe. With slight differences, the rhetorical structure of the three longest poems utilizes the foreground-background pattern of many of the poems found in *Hours* and especially *Shadows*. "The Grapes" dramatizes the tragedies of ordinary people who live out their small lives against a media-packaged backdrop of travel, stardom, and metropoli whose tantalizing grapes seem intentionally dangled just out of their reach. "The Short End" chronicles the demystification, for one promising and lovely girl, of that sacrosanct, one-mold-fits-all institution, marriage. Speaking the thoughts of a dry brain in a dry season, the effete voice of "The Venetian Vespers" is owned by one who might have "made it" in this tawdry world that hawks fulfillment like a televangelist. Each of the major poems contains an epiphanic moment in which the protagonist realizes the horrifying littleness of his or her life.

The speaker of "The Grapes" is a modern-day female counterpart of J. Alfred Prufrock, "a chambermaid," whose diction is a bit too elevated to be believed, of the *Hôtel de l' Univers et Déjeuner*. She views the really good life as always being on the opposite slope (the grass is always greener there), at the *Beau Rivage*, where her fantasy lover, the bellboy Marc-Antoine, "dreams of a young millionairess, / Beautiful, spoiled and ardent" who will rescue him from his contemptible life. "Perhaps it shall all come to pass. Such things have happened." Aging, the chambermaid acknowledges that the time is past when, Cinderella-like, she may be carried to exotic castles by a Prince Charming. She looks at grapes in a bowl and, pitifully, sees in this objective correlative that the moment of her greatness has flickered.

> ... And I seemed to know
> In my blood the meaning of sidereal time
> And know my little life had somehow crested.
> There was nothing for me now, nothing but years.

Like Prufrock's, her thoughts project themselves "as if a magic lantern threw the nerves in patterns on a screen":

> Reflections of the water dodged and swam
> In nervous incandescent filaments
> Over my blouse and up along the ceiling.

Like Prufrock saying, "I am not Prince Hamlet," the chambermaid recognizes she is no Cleopatra.

> My destiny was cast and Marc-Antoine

> Would not be called to play a part in it.
> His passion, his Dark Queen, he'd meet elsewhere.

The persona's necessarily vicarious life is symbolized by her favorite magazine, *Time*, in which "The rich and sleek of the international set / . . . get divorced / In a world so far removed from the rest of us / It almost seems arranged for our amusement," and more strikingly by the metaphor of the sun and two mountains, worked so as to evoke the woman's sense of the incredibly sad passage of time.

"The Short End" might well have used as epigraph Ambrose Bierce's definition of "love" in *The Devil's Dictionary*: "a temporary insanity curable by marriage." The poem records how loves turns bitter, its theme expressed by "the incontestable voice / Of someone who could not possibly be there," Miss McIntosh, Shirley's eleventh grade Latin teacher who visits her in a vision and explains that the Latin "'to love,' *amare*, / . . . also happens to be the word for 'bitter.'" Hecht's gloss to these lines reads, "strictly speaking it is the adverbial 'bitterly,' but this lapse is to be explained by the imperfect memory of a former student in an hour of stress."

Shirley Carson collects touristy pillows,

> . . . the largest
> assemblage of such pillows in the East:
> Pillows from Kennebunkport, balsam-scented
> And stuffed with woodchips, pillows from Coney Island
> Blazoned with Ferris Wheels and Roller Coasters,

Pillows that fart when sat on, tasselled pillows

From Old New Orleans, creole and redly carnal,

And what may be the gem of the collection,

From the New York World's Fair of Thirty-Nine,

Bearing a white Trylon and Perisphere,

Moderne, severe and thrilling, on the recto;

And on the verso in gold and blue italics

The Fair's motto: "A Century of Progress."

After the epic catalogue of Section I, the remainder of the poem takes pains to show that this century has been regressive or that its progress is mostly façade. The poem is also a compendium of cognominal puns that debase the lives of Shirley and Norman "Kit" Carson. The pillows soften "the hard edges of their lives" in this collisive world (Kit owns a body shop). At a convention during their newlywed year, a crass traveling salesman proposes toasts

To "good ol' Shirl an' Kit," names which he slurred

Both in pronunciation and disparagement

With an expansive, wanton drunkenness

That in its license seemed soberly planned

To increase by graduated steps until

Without seeming aware of what he was doing

He'd raise a toast to "good ol' Curl an' Shit."

This experience with traveling salesmen and their "wives," belatedly revealed as prostitutes, initiates Shirley into the opposing worlds of male and female. In the world in which "masculine snort and self-assertion," "cigars and bets and locker rooms" have "nothing to do with damask and chandeliers," Shirley gets "the short end" of the stick, as the title implies. Her husband's jobs, then as traveling salesman and now as mechanic, lead to dead ends. In the barren marriage, the pillows function as surrogate children.

Although the poem does not belabor the point, Shirley's tragedy is in part due to the impossible romantic versions of the opposite sexes that American culture has created and sustains largely through advertising, especially the false advertising of *Playboy*'s photographically doctored centerfolds thumbtacked to the walls of Kit's body shop. In Section II, Shirley, now fatly alcoholic, recalls her "first, untainted months of marriage." At the Atlantic City convention, she was "Hopeful, adoring, and in return adored" by her husband. Waiting for "Her only Norman [to] be returned to her" from his motivational meetings, she made "Forays on the interminable vista / Of the boardwalk," which at first symbolizes unspent potential: "it seemed to stretch away / In hazy diminution. . . ."

"Or so it seemed in prospect." In retrospect, its cheap carney world represents the freak sideshow air of lower-class pop culture seen most evidently at the present in "professional" wrestling.

> Such was this place, a hapless rural seat
> And sandy edge of the Truck Garden State,
> The dubious North American Paradise.

Locating the allusion in *Paradise Lost*, Hecht's gloss indicates the boardwalk's parody of Eden. To an ingénue like Shirley, at least, the amusement park would be considered paradise. The gloss falls short of revealing the root irony of "paradise," the Greek *paradeisos*, an enclosed park.

Section IV concerns the "LIVE ENTOMBMENT" of George Rose, archetypal embodiment of fame-hungry con artists of middle-America who do Guinnessy things for a brief moment in the spotlight of a Barnum and Bailey world. Early in their marriage, when Shirley is apparently on a road trip with Kit in his traveling salesman capacity, the couple stop at the roadside attraction. A glass aperture allows the curious to see the entombed. A poster records the obvious lie: "'George Rose / Is eager to preserve his solitude.'" Like other transparent financial ventures in the name of God or charity, believed mostly by the obtuse and psychologically needy, this one delivers the goods before getting to the punch line: "'Donations will be gratefully accepted.'" Intuitively repulsed by the display, Shirley turns from

> . . . the little clustered knot
> Of humankind around that sheet of glass,
> Like flies around a dish of sweetened water,
> And focuse[s] intently on what [lies] before her,

that is, a barren, retrograde landscape emblematic of her future:

> The air sang with the cold of empty caves,
> Of mildew, cobwebs, slug and maggot life.

The phrase "Like flies around a dish of sweetened water" is Hecht's indictment of what the American populace ingests as entertainment. Shirley's realization of her limitations leads to an anxiety-generated vision in which her life's homework is assigned by her high school Latin teacher. Such gripping recognition of the individual's littleness causes in others a similar psychic slippage that allows a projected inner-voice, apocalyptic and prophetic, to declare their unique calling. They see in tortilla shells the face of Jesus, or Jesus himself tells them to kill their babies or themselves in isolated religious communities of South America, or they become Jesus and destroy Michaelangelo's *Pietà*, or Holden Caulfield and kill John Lennon. Shirley is told to "humbly prepare" herself "For the coming resurrection of George Rose," whose surname, as a verb, prophesies his ascension, and, as a noun, indicates the conventional Christ-symbol or perhaps Dante's Mystic Rose.

In Section V, Shirley, at three A.M. in the present, is fixed on "a full-page color ad" in *The New Yorker*, the type of romantic ad in part responsible for ruining her life. She sees a lady "and a gentleman / . . . / Standing behind her, his arms about her waist," and imagines herself in his arms. Depicted in the rhetoric as a Moderne Adam and Eve, they have "all Fifth Avenue stretched out before them / in Élysée prospectus. . . ." In "the carriage lantern on the hansom cab," Shirley sees a "pure kernel / Of fire" and in it "The figure *redivivus* of George Rose, / Arisen, youthful, strong and roseate. . . ."

> She sees the last thing she will ever see:
> The purest red there is, passional red,
> Fire-engine red, the red of Valentines,
> Of which she is herself the howling center.

An earlier passage informs these last lines of the poem: "She would sit up late, smoking and drinking." Her cigarette ashes have apparently touched off a fire among her pillows. The flames' red is appropriately "Fire-engine red" and, symbolizing her romantically tragic life, "the red of Valentines."

"The Venetian Vespers" is the phylogenic story of Western Civilization recapitulated in the ontogeny of an effete "twentieth century infidel" whose language is laced with inescapable Christian allusions. The son of emigrant parents from Lawrence, Massachusetts, the persona, who calls himself "a viral parasite," has moved to Venice to live out his last days. Echoes of *The Wasteland*, "Prufrock," the "Preludes," and especially "Gerontion" underscore the persona's emptiness in the midst of a bountiful world.[3] Sick to death, single, heirless, he has been failed or rejected by his mother, father, uncle, country, and faith.

The updated, more sophisticated, but just as vacuous Prufrock reflects, from morning to evening of a single day, on his worthless life. Prufrock asks, "And how should I begin?" Hecht's significantly nameless speaker finds difficulty beginning the rehearsal of his life. After several false starts, he says, "Well, yes. Any of these might somehow serve / As departure point" (lines 41-42). By line 480, he is still asking himself, "Where to begin?"

The vacuity of the persona's life is concretized in objective correlatives: "shattered amber / That held a pint of rye," "The carapace / Of a dried beetle," "A broken orange crate," "chips of brick," "the endless flapping of one window-shade," and, most telling, Venetian bottle-breaking, the "space-saving work / Of the young men who run the garbage scows." These castaway bottles "Await what is at once their liquidation / And resurrection in the glory holes / Of the Murano furnaces," but the persona, who has made a fiasco (Italian, "flask") of his life ("*Ho fatto un fiasco*, which is to say, / I've made a sort of bottle of my life") can experience no such recycling of his wasted life, nor can he rescind his actions in the manner of the Keystone Cops movie of Section I, "Which for the sake of the children in the house / The projectionist has ventured to run backwards."

More generally, the poem is a lamentation on the indignities of old age and the fear of insanity.

> O that the soul should tie its shoes, the mind
> Should wash its hands in a sink, that a small grain
> Of immortality should fit itself
> With dentures. We slip down by grades and degrees,
> Lapses of memory, the vacant eye
> And spittled lip, by soiled humiliations
> Of mind and body into the last ditch. . . .

The persona's reductive musings compare human life to a "genetic swamp" in which survival of the fittest reigns as ultimate law.

> Blessed be the unseen micro-organisms,
> For without doubt they shall inherit the earth.
> Their generations shall be as the sands of the sea.
> I am the dying host by which they live;
> In me they dwell and thrive and have their being.

The persona's references to Matthew 5, Jeremiah 33.22, and Acts 17.28 point to his past search for an active morality, though his passive goodness is finally grounded on a *via negativa:*

> My efforts at their best are negative:
> A poor attempt not to hurt anyone,
> A goal which, in the very nature of things,
> Is ludicrous because impossible.

This morality of staying out of the way was instilled in him by both emigrant parents and surrogate parents. Slightly altered lines from "Gerontion" further disclose his defaulted goodness: "Thus virtues, it is said, are forced upon us / By our own impudent crimes." Even the idea of immortality he interprets as no more than the ultimate self-assertive attempt at survival.

> . . . There is something selfish in the self,
> The cell's craving for perpetuity,
> The sperm's ignorant hope, the animal's rule
> Of haunch and sinew, testicle and groin
> That refers all things whatever, near and far,
> To one's own needs or fantasized desires.

In this inventory and re-view of his life, we discover that the persona once cared about his fellows, "was an Aid Man, / A Medic with an infantry company, / Who because of [his] refusal to bear arms / Was constrained to bear the wounded and the dead / From under enemy fire. . . ." We learn that even his conscientious objection was merely another manifestation of his noncommittal attitude towards life. At the writing of the poem, he regards "Life as a spectator sport," as the many windows through which he looks indicate, and has abandoned even his country.

Yet his is not a soul utterly lost. Musing on the ease with which movie characters can annul their mistakes by a simple reverse of the projector, he allows his suppressed compassion to emerge in a brief but heartfelt moment.

> Something profoundly soiled, pointlessly hurt
> And beyond cure in us yearns for this costless
> Ablution, this impossible reprieve,
> Unpurchased at a scaffold, free, bequeathed
> As rain upon the just and unjust,
> As in the fall of mercy, unconstrained,
> Upon the poor, infected place beneath.

In the poem's last lines, he may in fact be redeemed. Looking out of his window at the spendthrift colors of sunset and extravagant shapes of clouds "That visibly rebuke our stinginess," he, as mere spectator, is ravished by the saving splendor of nature.

> . . . I look and look,
> As though I could be saved simply by looking—
> I, who have never earned my way, who am
> No better than a viral parasite,
> Or the lees of the Venetian underworld,
> Foolish and muddled in my later years,
> Who was never even at one time a wise child.

That phrase "As though" leaves room for us to doubt the persona's experience, but Hecht's own wonder at the world's splendor indicates at least the possiblity of his salvation.

AFTERWORD

So much of this study has been concerned with showing Hecht's indebtedness to Auden, Yeats, Ransom, the Metaphysicals, and others that it is important to point out the merit of his work apart from his creditors. What Hecht does as well as or better than these colossi is give us in particularity the palpable extravagance of the world. In nearly every poem, he refuses to sail to Byzantium.

What is most striking about the poems of Anthony Hecht is on the one hand their philosophical quarrel with the-world-as-it-is and on the other a corrective reveling in nature's splendor. In separate poems, the world's paradisal grandeur ("'Gladness of the Best'") balances its hellish barrenness ("A Hill"). But if we can say "Yeatsian" or "Audenesque," what constitutes the distinctive "Hechtian" poem? Throughout his work, as in the early "Discourse Concerning Temptation," Hecht simultaneously celebrates and laments the ambiguous nature of the world. The Hechtian poem, then, holds the tension of two antithetical worlds colliding: "Alceste in the Wilderness," "Harangue," "Third Avenue in Sunlight," "The End of the Weekend," "The Odds," "The Ghost in the Martini," and "'More Light! More Light!'" Other poems bound by the contraries of stasis and flux will be remembered: "'Dichtung und Wahrheit'" and "Swan Dive"; as will those that convey transcendence: "After the Rain" and "'Gladness of the Best'"; and those that create memorable though pathetic characters: "The Short End" and "The Venetian Vespers."

How Hecht incorporates his themes is also distinctive. In his essay "On the Methods and Ambitions of Poetry," Hecht has said that "art serves to ... invite ... a state of aesthetic contemplation." He observes that "There is a difference between looking at a beautiful landscape and looking at a beautiful painting of the same landscape."[1] By filtering his subject through a cultured persona, a painting, or a landscape, and through rhymes and formal stanzas, Hecht forces us to see the poem more for its aesthetic symmetry than for its "message," which is not to say that his poems are without moral import. This screening effect is the more evident when as readers of Hecht we must contemplate a poem of a painting of a landscape ("At the Frick," "The Place of Pain in the Universe," "A Poem for Julia," "'Gladness of the Best'").

What this study has also tried to show is how strongly Hecht's aesthetic stances rely on Ransom's, an influence he freely confesses. How thoroughly he has incorporated the ideas and terminology of the New Critics into that of classical literary theory and personal transcendental beliefs is borne out in a passage from the "Ambitions of Poetry" essay:

> The poem wishes to pay its homage to the natural world, from which it derives and which it strives to imitate. And there is in nature a superfluity, an excess of texture which plays no necessary part in the natural economy. It may be that the bees are attracted by the color of the rose; but the rose is capable of so many exquisite gradations and modulations of color that they must surely exceed any practical end. And nature, or the power behind it, is full of such fine excesses, and finds occasion, in some famous words, "to cause it to rain on the earth where no man is; on the wilderness wherein there is no man; to

satisfy the desolate waste ground; and to cause the bud of the tender herb to spring forth." Systems of theology refer this richness to some end. Poetry is sometimes more hesitant, but wishes to register such splendor, to imitate it, and presently to assign to it . . . a sense of purposiveness.[2]

I do not know of a poet who more liberally scatters before us the world's diadems than Anthony Hecht, yet he is cognizant of the dark side, that "Pleasure and pain [are] necessary twins," and if he has made peace with the world it is an apprehensive peace. I close with his words.

Often enough [a poet's] configurations are based precisely on tension, and on tension at a terrible and perilous pitch. They invite within the world of their discourse our sweetest triumphs and deepest desolations, and exhibit to us freshly and frighteningly all the terrible violence which may be implied in the formula of the bomb. . . . And at last, in allowing us to contemplate, even within a single poem, such diversity of experience, both the good and the bad, brought into tenuous balance through all the manifold devices of art, the spirit is set at ease by a kind of katharsis, in which we are brought to acknowledge that this is the way things are, and by which is recovered for us at the end the inexhaustible plenitude of the world.[3]

NOTES AND REFERENCES

Introduction

1. Anthony Hecht, "Masters of Unpleasantness," *New York Times Book Review* 7 February 1982: 3, 25. Unless otherwise noted, subsequent quotations are taken from this source.

2. Paul Desruisseaux, "Hecht Concludes 'Very Agreeable Adventure' as Library of Congress's Poetry Consultant," *Chronicle of Higher Education* 9 May 1984: 8.

3. Anthony Hecht, "John Crowe Ransom," *American Scholar* 49 (Summer 1980): 379-83. Unless otherwise noted, subsequent quotations are taken from this source.

4. Wendy Smith, "Anthony and Helen Hecht," *Publishers Weekly* 18 July 1986: 70-71.

5. Donald Davie, "Book Reviews," rev. of *Stones*, *Shenandoah* (Autumn 1956): 44.

6. Of the difference in style and content of his first two volumes, Hecht has said, "The subject matter [of *Stones*], in fact, didn't have a pressing, immediate need for me; I'd write about anything that came to hand. In contrast, many of the poems in *The Hard Hours* are about things that had enormous emotional importance to me; I was prepared to attack them, whether they came out technically perfect or not." Philip I. Gerber and Robert J. Gemmett, eds., "An Interview with Anthony Hecht," (With Gregory Fitz Gerald and William Heyen) *Mediterranean Review* 1.3 (1971): 6. *Hours* is written in what Donald Sheehan calls "Hecht's relaxed middle style." "Varieties of Technique: Seven Recent Books of American Poetry," rev. of *Hours*, *Contemporary Literature* 10.2 (Spring 1969): 301.

7. Although I see the variety in *Shadows* as a virtue, Steven Madoff says, "Hecht's present stylistic difficulties can be seen as a confusion of poetic realities: his predecessors' versus his own. This confusion is largely responsible for the unevenness present in *Millions of Strange Shadows*." "The Poet at Cross Purposes," *The Nation* 3 September 1977: 190.

8. Vernon Shetley, "Take But Degree Away," rev. of *Vespers*, *Poetry* 137.5 (February 1981): 297-8.

9. "Masters of Unpleasantness," *New York Times Book Review* 3. Eleven years before, Hecht said, "At the time I started to write, I felt that modern fiction

had greatly usurped the devices of poetry, that one taught a story by James Joyce, or a novel by Flaubert as though it were a lyric poem. And these works had very much the concision, the deftness and the unity of form and language that you expect of a lyric poem. They also had the advantage of narrative; while, in a way, lyric poems were dwindling down to nothing but ditties. So, when I began, I wanted somehow to repossess some of the interest in drama that comes from a narrative, with a potential working out of a story and its implications." Gerber 8.

10. "Envoi," *The Yale Review* 76.1 (Autumn 1986): 127.

11. John Crowe Ransom, "Poetry: I, The Formal Analysis," *Kenyon Review* 9 (Summer 1947): 436-56; reprt. in *Selected Essays of John Crowe Ransom*, eds. Thomas Daniel Young and John Hindle (Baton Rouge: Louisiana State University Press, 1984) 197.

12. Thomas Daniel Young, "The Evolution of Ransom's Critical Theory: Image and Idea," *The New Criticism and After*, ed. Thomas Daniel Young (Charlottesville: University Press of Virginia, 1976): 34.

Chapter One

1. In 1971, Hecht said, "I felt that about half [the poems in *Stones*] were worth preserving. I don't know why I disqualified the others. I guess I didn't like them well enough." Philip I. Gerber and Robert J. Gemmett, eds., "An Interview with Anthony Hecht," (With Gregory Fitz Gerald and William Heyen) *Mediterranean Review* 1.3 (1971): 5.

2. Several critics have noticed the foreground-background technique, including Irvin Ehrenpreis and Peter Scupham, who says, "Hecht's brocades are not still tapestries but swaying curtains: tentative or suggestive drop-scenes leading to the surprising human event after we have been entranced into watching, feeling, waiting." Peter Scupham, "Grisaille and Millefleurs," *Poetry Review* 76.3 (October 1986): 11. Irvin Ehrenpreis, "At the Poles of Poetry," rev. of *Shadows*, *New York Review of Books* 17 August 1978: 48-49.

3. Anthony Hecht, *Obbligati* (New York: Atheneum-Macmillan, 1986) 290-91.

4. H. W. Janson, *History of Art*, revised ed. (Englewood Cliffs: Prentice-Hall, Inc., 1974) 341-2.

5. John Crowe Ransom, "Wanted: An Ontological Critic," *The New Criticism*

(New Directions: 1941; Westport, CT: Greenwood Press, 1979) 306. For the fuller theoretical discussion, see sections five and six of "Wanted" (chapter four) and especially Ransom's brief but acute practical application of the theory to Andrew Marvell's "To His Coy Mistress."

6. Those whose tastes run to the unadorned have accused Hecht of "dandyism" [George Hemphill, "Anthony Hecht's Nunnery of Art," *Perspective* 12.4 (1962): 166] and "connoisseurship and preciosity" [Richard Wilbur, "Urgency and Artifice," *New York Times Book Review* 4 April 1954: 12]. His verse has been derided as "lexiconish" [Calvin Bedient, "New Confessions," *Sewanee Review* 88.3 (Summer 1980): 199] and praised as "exuberant topiary" [Richard Howard, *Alone With America* (New York: Atheneum-Macmillan, 1980) 199].

7. Anthony Hecht, letter to Norman German, 27 July 1982.

8. John Crowe Ransom, "Poetry: A Note in Ontology," *American Review* 3 (May 1934): 172-200; reprt. in *Selected Essays of John Crowe Ransom*, eds. Thomas Daniel Young and John Hindle (Baton Rouge: Louisiana State University Press, 1984) 76-77.

9. Ransom, "Wanted: An Ontological Critic," *The New Criticism* 291.

10. Compare Ransom's comment in "Forms and Citizens": "The fierce drives of the animals, whether human or otherwise, are only towards a *kind* of thing, the indifferent instance of a universal, and not some private irreplaceable thing. All the nouns at this stage are common nouns." "A Poem Nearly Anonymous: The Poet and His Formal Tradition," *American Review* 1 (September 1933): 444-67; reprt. in *Selected Essays of John Crowe Ransom* 63.

11. Richard C. Robey, gen. ed, *Diary of Samuel Sewall*, 3 vols. (New York: Arno Press, 1972) 3: 270.

12. *Diary of Samuel Sewall* 3: 267.

13. *Diary of Samuel Sewall* 3: 267.

14. *Diary of Samuel Sewall* 3: 272.

15. However, Hayden Carruth calls most of the poems from *Stones* and some from *Hours* "essentially contrivances; learned, allusive, skillful, but hollow; by which I mean they are like shells within which the felt experience is loose and unsupported. . . ." "Critic of the Month: I," rev. of *Hours*, *Poetry* 112.6 (September 1968): 424.

16. Some critics think there is no relation between subject matter and theme in these poems: "Nothing is so immediately Audenesque about his poems as their insolently perfunctory attitude to subject matter. 'Think of a subject, and verify it.'

Doubtless at all times indifferent poems have been written to this recipe." Donald
Davie, "Book Reviews," rev. of *Stones, Shenandoah* 8.1 (Autumn 1956): 43.

17. Richard Howard says Hecht's "first book is obsessed by an imagery of
decline from some original standard of possibility, by the knowledge that if we are
to return at all to the God-given Unity we fell from, it must be by some process (and
thereby utilizing the temporal) of impurity. . . ." *Alone With America* 196.

18. Peter Scupham notes the poem's likness to Erasmus Darwin's "The
Botanic Garden" (1792). "Grisaille and Millefleurs" 12.

19. Hecht, *Obbligati* 41.

20. David R. Coffin, *The Villa d' Este at Tivoli* (Princeton: Princeton University
Press, 1960) 70, 92, 5. See especially chapters 2, "The Gardens and Fountains," and
5, "The Villa's Symbolism and Pirro Ligorio." An uncommendable side of
Ligorio's personality is that he "showed no respect for private property, that he had
owners imprisoned or banished when they opposed excavation on their property,
and that he stripped the churches of antiquities" (8). A neat irony is that a Cardinal
Alessandro added a "very beautiful fountain" to the gardens (104). The maiden
name of Hecht's wife is D'Alessandro.

21. Coffin 95.

22. The quoted words are from "Wanted: An Ontological Critic," *The New
Criticism* 281. Ashley Brown says, "It is tempting to pursue the wit of this stanza
in several directions, and no doubt some readers have taken it as a *jeu d' esprit* of
the New Criticism (Brooks's paradox, Tate's tension, Warren's pure and impure
poetry, etc.) long before now. But the stanza should direct our attention to Marvell's
Garden (the important literary reference), hence back to Eden itself." "The Poetry
of Anthony Hecht," *Ploughshares* 4.3 (1978): 14.

23. William H. Pritchard, *Frost: A Literary Life Reconsidered* (New York:
Oxford University Press, 1984) 236.

24. Pritchard 238.

25. Compare Yeats' "I spit into the face of Time / That has transfigured me,"
from "The Lamentation of the Old Pensioner."

26. Donald Louis Hill, *Richard Wilbur* (New York: Twayne Publishers, Inc.,
1967) 99, 178.

27. Laurence Lieberman contends that "Hecht's most consistently masterful
device is to juxtapose stories from history, ancient and contemporary (or scenes
from his personal life, present and past), generating a powerful religious and
political moral from collision between them." "Recent Poetry in Review: Risks and

Faiths," rev. of *Hours*, *Yale Review* 57.4 (1968): 603.

28. Steven Madoff reports that at Hecht's "The Education of the Poet" Guggenheim lecture in 1977, the poet claimed two great influences: music and "his experience as an infantryman in World War II which he survived with the most profound ambivalence in knowing that his own life was saved in the Pacific Theatre by the dropping of the atomic bomb." "The Poet at Cross Purposes," rev. of *Shadows*, *The Nation* 3 September 1977: 188.

29. Definitions taken from *Webster's New International Dictionary* and *American Heritage Dictionary*.

30. If we are to believe Hecht's commentary in the mock-scholarly introduction to *Jiggery-Pokery*, then the dactylic dimeter one-word line "Schistosomiasis," the poet's "crestfallen" apologetics (not apology) about its being in an iambic poem, and the face-saving suggestion of a friend all combined in the genesis of the Double Dactyl verse form popularized by Hecht and John Hollander. Introduction, *Jiggery-Pokery: A Compendium of Double Dactyls* (New York: Atheneum-Macmillan, 1983) 17-18.

31. Paul Desruisseaux, "Hecht Concludes 'Very Agreeable Adventure' as Library of Congress's Poetry Consultant," *Chronicle of Higher Education* 9 May 1984: 8.

32. Desruisseaux 8.

33. Tony Hecht, "To a Soldier Killed in Germany," *Kenyon Review* 9.2 (Spring 1946): 223-24.

Chapter Two

1. Jonathan Keates, "Vault Echoes," rev. of *Vespers*, *The Spectator* 244.7922 (10 May 1980): 24.

2. Philip Gerber and Robert Gemmett, eds., "An Interview with Anthony Hecht," (With Gregory Fitz Gerald and William Heyen) *Mediterranean Review* 1.3 (1971): 5.

3. Of the poem's genesis, Hecht has stated, "The poem derives, in fact, from an anecdote that was told to me by Ted Hughes, the English poet and husband of Sylvia Plath, about an experience he once had." Gerber, "An Interview with Anthony Hecht" 4.

4. Marjorie Perloff calls the "great black presence" a "rapacious bat" while

Gregory Fitz Gerald calls it an owl. Marjorie Perloff, "The Hard Hours," rev. of
Hours, The Far Point 2 (1969): 46. Gerber, "An Interview with Anthony Hecht"
5. Several facts favor the owl camp. North American bats are almost exclusively
fruit- and insect-eaters. North America's largest bat is only five and one-half inches
long, while its owls reach two feet in height and a wingspan of over four feet. The
bird in the poem has the "golden eyes" typical of owls. Also, bats eat their meals
in flight and do not bring them "home."

   5. Hecht's thoughts on the dream indicate the poem's larger significance:
"The modern world is filled with similar illustrations of cruelty. So that in my own
mind, and, I should hope in the reader's mind also, this is not merely a poem about
something that happened to a Roman emperor a long time ago, but a vision of the
kind of mental process that results in contemporary cruelty and barbarity." Gerber,
"An Interview with Anthony Hecht" 7.

   6. Anthony Hecht, letter to Norman German, 17 September 1982.

   7. Definitions taken from *The Oxford English Dictionary*.

   8. My assumption is that Hecht's formal verse partakes of ritual. Ransom's
comments on the function of religious ritual may further inform the reader
concerning the formal verse of "Rites and Ceremonies": "The religious society
exists in order to serve the man in this crisis [grieving for the dead]. Freed from his
desolation by its virtue, he is not obliged now to run and throw himself upon the
body in an ecstasy of grief, nor to go apart and brood upon the riddle of mortality,
which may be the way of madness. His action is through the form of a pageant of
grief. . . . His own grief expands, is lightened, no longer has to be explosive or
obsessive. A sort of by-product of this formal occasion, we need not deny, is his
grateful sense that his community supports him in a dreadful hour. But what
interests us rather is the fact that his preoccupation with the deadness of the body
is broken by his participation in the pageantry, and his bleak situation elaborated
with such rich detail that it becomes massive, substantial, and sufficient." "Forms
and Citizens," *Selected Essays of John Crowe Ransom* 62-63.

   9. Brad Leithauser has correctly noted, for instance, that the last six stanzas
of Section II, "The Fire Sermon," faithfully reproduce the form of those in George
Herbert's "Deniall." "Poet for a Dark Age," *New York Review of Books* 13 February
1986: 12. Hecht even borrows three full lines from the poem: "O that thou shouldst
give dust a tongue / To crie to thee, / And then not heare it crying!"

   10. In "Black Boy in the Dark," from *Shadows*, Hecht resorts to the Whitman
lines with direct acknowledgement: "We were there, / We suffered, we were

Whitman."

11. Mircea Eliade, *The Myth of the Eternal Return: or, Cosmos and History*, trans. Willard R. Trask (Princeton: Princeton University Press, 1974) 96.

12. Eliade 96.

13. Eliade 97-8.

14. Northrop Frye, *Anatomy of Criticism* (Princeton: Princeton University Press, 1973) 119-120.

15. Eliade 21, 53.

16. Eliade 152.

17. Daniel Hoffman, "Poets: Dissidents from Schools," in *Harvard Guide to Contemporary American Writers*, ed. Daniel Hoffman (Cambridge: Harvard University Press, 1979) 582.

18. Hoffman 583.

19. Eliade 47.

20. Leithauser 11.

Chapter Three

1. The phrase is from "'Dichtung und Wahrheit,'" from *Shadows*.

2. Baron Joseph van der Elst, *The Last Flowering of the Middle Ages* (Garden City, NY: Doubleday, Doran and Company, Inc., 1955) 124.

3. Concerning the discernible patterns of history, Hecht has said, "... the more I read of history, the more it seems that the same problems present themselves in different ways. I think this recognition accounts for some of the historical references in my own poetry." Gerber, "An Interview with Anthony Hecht" 7.

4. Van der Elst 124.

5. Hecht's anti-war sentiments were voiced in the 1971 interview with Gregory Fitz Gerald and William Heyen: "As a poet, the danger of writing about what's going on in Viet Nam—a war which I wholly disapprove of—is that I might end up merely getting up on a soap box and being shrill and hortatory." Gerber, "An Interview with Anthony Hecht" 7.

6. Anthony Hecht, letter to Norman German, 27 July 1982.

7. Ralph Waldo Emerson, *The Collected Works of Ralph Waldo Emerson*, eds. Robert E. Spiller and Alfred R. Ferguson (Cambridge: The Belknap Press of the Harvard University Press, 1971) 1: 27.

8. Emerson 1: 7, 11.

9. "When the particular detail of the flowers is mentioned, I've resorted to an allusion to the 'all-over' floral patterns famous in Gobelin tapestries, but equally to be found, in terms of decorative and patterned design, in illuminations." Anthony Hecht, letter to Norman German, 26 December 1984. In the same letter, Hecht calls this a "conflation of images."

10. George Herbert, *The Essential Herbert*, ed. Anthony Hecht (New York: The Ecco Press, 1987) 9-10.

11. Emerson 1: 27-28.

12. Emerson 1: 27.

13. Ransom, "Wanted: An Ontological Critic," *The New Criticism* 281.

14. Focusing on formal concerns, note that Hecht's precise artistry dictates that if he rhymes "most" with "ghosts," he must rhyme "taste" with "wastes." Similarly, because "coins" rhymes with "undermines" in stanza three, it rhymes with "signs" in stanza six. However, this fastidiousness does not prevent him from rhyming "over" with "river" in stanza two or "shadowless" with "grass" in stanza four.

15. Hecht, *Obbligati* 12.

16. Hecht, *Obbligati* 11-12, italics added.

17. Ransom, "Poetry: A Note in Ontology," *Selected Essays* 83.

18. Emerson 1: 23.

19. G. E. Murray has also noted the poem's blend of humor and gloom: "More than ever before . . . humor now infiltrate[s] Anthony Hecht's vision. The addition is a blessing, particularly evidenced by the superb poem 'The Ghost in the Martini,' a wildly funny, yet bracing look at the hollow retreat into middle age." Untitled review of *Shadows*, *Georgia Review* 31.4 (Winter 1977): 964.

20. Samuel Enoch Stumph, *Socrates to Sartre: A History of Philosophy*, 2nd ed. (New York: McGraw-Hill Book Company, 1975) 449-53.

Chapter Four

1. Paul Desruisseaux, "Hecht Concludes 'Very Agreeable Adventure' as Library of Congress's Poetry Consultant," *Chronicle of Higher Education* 9 May 1984: 8.

2. Brad Leithauser, "Poet for a Dark Age," *New York Review of Books* 13 February 1986: 12.

3. Vernon Shetley also notes the poem's resemblance to "Gerontion." "Take But Degree Away," rev. of *Vespers*, *Poetry* 137.5 (February 1981): 298.

Afterword

1. Anthony Hecht, "On the Methods and Ambitions of Poetry," *Hudson Review* 18.4 (Winter 1965-66): 490.
2. "Ambitions" 492.
3. "Ambitions" 505.

SELECTED BIBLIOGRAPHY

PRIMARY SOURCES

1. Poetry

The Hard Hours. 1967. New York: Atheneum-Macmillan, 1981.

Hecht, Anthony. "Envoi." *Yale Review* 76.1 (Autumn 1986): 127.

Hecht, Tony. "To a Soldier Killed in Germany." *Kenyon Review* 9.2 (Spring 1947): 223-24.

Millions of Strange Shadows. 1977. New York: Atheneum-Macmillan, 1980.

A Summoning of Stones. New York: The Macmillan Company, 1954.

The Venetian Vespers. 1979. New York: Atheneum-Macmillan, 1980.

2. Criticism, Commentary, Editions, Reviews

"A Few Green Leaves." *Sewanee Review* 67 (Autumn 1959): 568-71. Tribute to Allen Tate.

Hecht, Anthony, and John Hollander, eds. *Jiggery-Pokery: A Compendium of Double Dactyls*. New York: Atheneum-Macmillan, 1983.

Herbert, George. *The Essential Herbert*. Ed. Anthony Hecht. New York: The Ecco Press, 1987.

"John Crowe Ransom." *American Scholar* 49 (Summer 1980): 379-383.

"Masters of Unpleasantness." *New York Times Book Review* 7 February 1982: 3, 25.

Obbligati: Essays in Criticism. New York: Atheneum-Macmillan, 1986.

"On the Methods and Ambitions of Poetry." *Hudson Review* 18.4 (Winter 1965-66): 489-505.

3. Interviews

Desruisseaux, Paul. "Hecht Concludes 'Very Agreeable Adventure' as Library of Congress's Poetry Consultant." *Chronicle of Higher Education* 9 May 1984: 5, 8.

Gerber, Philip I., and Robert J. Gemmett, eds. "An Interview with Anthony Hecht." With Gregory Fitz Gerald and William Heyen. *Mediterranean Review* 1.3 (1971): 3-9.

Smith, Wendy. "Anthony & Helen Hecht." *Publishers Weekly* 18 July 1986: 70-71.

SECONDARY SOURCES

Bedient, Calvin. "New Confessions." Rev. of *Vespers. Sewanee Review* 88.3 (Summer 1980): 474-77.

Bennet, Joseph. "Recent Verse." Rev. of *Stones. Hudson Review* 7.2 (Summer 1954): 306-308.

Berry, Duc de. *The* Très Riches Heures *of Jean, Duke of Berry.* Introduction and Legends by Jean Longnon and Raymond Cazelles. Preface by Millard Meiss. New York: George Braziller, Inc., 1969.

Bloom, Harold. "Harold Bloom on Poetry." Rev. of *Shadows. New Republic* 26 November 1977: 25.

Brown, Ashley. "The Poetry of Anthony Hecht." *Ploughshares* 4.3 (1978): 9-24.

Carruth, Hayden. "Critic of the Month: I." Rev. of *Hours. Poetry* 112.6 (September 1968): 424.

Coffin, David R. *The Villa d'Este at Tivoli.* Princeton: Princeton University Press, 1960.

Davie, Donald. "Book Reviews." Rev. of *Stones. Shenandoah* 8.1 (Autumn 1956): 43-44.

_____. "The Twain Not Meeting." Rev. of *Vespers. Parnassus* 8.1 (1980): 84-91.

Donoghue, Denis. "Millions of Strange Shadows." Rev. of *Shadows. New York Times Book Review* 27 March 1977: 6-7.

Ehrenpreis, Irvin. "At the Poles of Poetry." Rev. of *Shadows. New York Review of Books* 17 August 1978: 48-49.

Eliade, Mircea. *The Myth of the Eternal Return: or, Cosmos and History.* Trans. Willard R. Trask. Princeton: Princeton University Press, 1974.

Emerson, Ralph Waldo. *The Collected Works of Ralph Waldo Emerson.* Eds. Robert E. Spiller, Introduction, and Alfred R. Ferguson. Vol. I: *Nature, Addresses, and Lectures.* Cambridge: The Belknap Press of the Harvard University Press, 1971.

Flint, R. W. "Poets of the '50s." Rev. of *Stones. Partisan Review* 21:6 (Nov-Dec 1954): 679-81.

Frye, Northrop. *Anatomy of Criticism: Four Essays.* Princeton: Princeton University Press, 1973.

Garfitt, Roger. "Contrary Attractions." Rev. of *Vespers. Times Literary Supplement* 30 May 1980: 623.

Graham, Desmond. "The Lying Art?" Rev. of *Shadows*. *Stand* 20.1 (1978-79): 65-71.

Greiner, Donald J., gen. ed. *Dictionary of Literary Biography: American Poets Since World War II*, Vol. 5, Part 1. Detroit: Book Tower, 1980.

Hemphill, George. "Anthony Hecht's Nunnery of Art." *Perspective* 12.4 (1962): 163-171.

Hoffman, Daniel. "Poetry: Dissidents from Schools," 581-86, in *Harvard Guide to Contemporary American Writing*. Ed. Daniel Hoffman. Cambridge: Harvard University Press, 1979.

Howard, Richard. "Anthony Hecht: 'What Do We Know of Lasting Since the Fall?'" 195-208, in *Alone With America: Essays on the Art of Poetry in the United States since 1950*. New York: Atheneum-Macmillan, 1980.

Johnson, Richard A. "Summer Knowledge, Hard Hours." Rev. of *Hours*. *Sewanee Review* 76.4 (Autumn 1968): 682-85.

Joost, Nicholas. "Hecht's 'Ostia Antica.'" *Explicator* 20.2 (September 1961): item 14.

Keates, Jonathan. "Vault Echoes." Rev. of *Vespers*. *Spectator* 244.7922 (10 May 1980): 23-24.

Leithauser, Brad. "Poet for a Dark Age." *New York Review of Books* 13 February 1986: 11-12, 14.

Lieberman, Laurence. "Recent Poetry in Review: Risks and Faiths." Rev. of *Hours*. *Yale Review* 57.4 (Summer 1968): 601-603.

McClatchy, J. D. "Summaries and Evidence." Rev. of *Vespers*. *Partisan Review* 47.4 (1980): 643-44.

Madoff, Steven. "The Poet at Cross Purposes." Rev. of *Shadows*. *The Nation* 3 September 1977: 188-90.

Malkoff, Karl, ed. *Crowell's Handbook of Contemporary Poetry*. New York: Thomas Y. Crowell Company, 1973.

Meredith, William. "Formal Effects." Rev. of *Hours*. *New York Times Book Review* 17 December 1967: 24-25.

Miller, Stephen. "A Poem by Anthony Hecht." *Spirit* 39.1 (1972): 8-11. Explication of "The Cost."

Mizener, Arthur. "Transformations." Rev. of *Stones*. *Kenyon Review* 16 (1954): 479-81.

Morris, Herbert. "After the Reading." *New England Review and Breadloaf Quarterly* 5.1-2 (Autumn-Winter 1982): 81-85. The epistolary poem, opening "Dear Mr. Hecht" and parodying Hecht's style and many of his poems, meditates on a 1951 photograph of the poet and ends with the amusing inquiry of "where foliage ends / and, against it, Anthony Hecht begins."

Murray, G. E. Review of *Shadows*. *Georgia Review* 31.4 (Winter 1977): 962-64.

O'Brien, Timothy D. "Hecht's 'The Dover Bitch.'" *Explicator* 44.2 (Winter 1986): 52-54.

Perloff, Marjorie. "The Hard Hours." Rev. of *Hours*. *The Far Point* 2 (1969): 45-51. A long assessment of Hecht's work asserting that "Hecht is not the major poet his admirers claim him to be."

Pettingell, Phoebe. "Anthony Hecht's Transmutations." Rev. of *Vespers*. *New Leader* 62.24 (17 December 1979): 22-23.

Pritchard, William H. *Frost: A Literary Life Reconsidered*. New York: Oxford University Press, 1984.

Ransom, John Crowe. *The New Criticism*. New Directions: 1941; Westport, CN: Greenwood Press, 1979.

_____. *Selected Essays of John Crowe Ransom*. Eds. Thomas Daniel Young and John Hindle. Baton Rouge: Louisiana State University Press, 1984.

Ricks, Christopher. "Poets Who Have Learned Their Trade." Rev. of *Vespers*. *New York Times Book Review* 2 December 1979: 1, 44-45.

Scupham, Peter. "Grisaille and Millefleurs." *Poetry Review* (London) 76.3 (October 1986): 9-12. An overview of Hecht's poetry in terms of its "pain and delight."

Sewall, Samuel. *Diary of Samuel Sewall: 1674-1729*. Research Library of Colonial Americana. Gen. Ed., Richard C. Robey. 3 Vols. New York: Arno Press, 1972.

Sheehan, Donald. "Varieties of Technique: Seven Recent Books of American Poetry." Rev. of *Hours*. *Contemporary Literature* 10.2 (Spring 1969): 298-301.

Shetley, Vernon. "Take But Degree Away." Rev. of *Vespers*. *Poetry* 137.5 (February 1981): 297-98.

"Unamerican Editions." Rev. of *Hours*. *Times Literary Supplement* 23 November 1967: 1106.

Van der Elst, Baron Joseph. *The Last Flowering of the Middle Ages*. Garden City: Doubleday, Doran and Company, Inc., 1955.

Vinson, James, ed. *Contemporary Poets*. 2nd ed. New York: St. Martin's Press, 1975.

Wilbur, Richard. "Urgency and Artifice." *New York Times Book Review* 4 April 1954: 12.

Young, Thomas Daniel, ed. *The New Criticism and After*. Charlottesville: University Press of Virginia, 1976.

Index

Glen Burns

GREAT POETS HOWL
A Study of Allen Ginsberg's Poetry, 1943–1955

European University Studies: Series XIV (Anglo-Saxon Language and Literature). Vol. 114
ISBN 0-8204-7761-6   540 pages   paperback sFr. 83.00

Recommended price – alterations reserved

Allen Ginsberg's *Howl* is a seminal document for the post-modernisms exfoliating out of World War II–much like T. S. Eliot's *Waste Land* for modernism. This study traces his formative development in time/space during years 1943 till mid-50s *Howl* breakthru of individual voice. (A concluding chapter sketches subsequent development up to *Plutonium Ode* 1978). Close-reading of individual poems is set within the context of biography and cultural politics showing growth of Ginsberg's poetics as adapted from William Carlos Williams' visions of ordinary mind, Whitman's expansiveness and comradeship, and Blake's politics of desire. As «revolt of sudras (untouchables) poet,» Ginsberg has concentrated language on marginal mankind so that poetic praxis folds into a dimension of visionary politics and poem becomes prophetic moment voiced against the paranoia of state terrorism. *Howl* is a key event in the struggle for freedom.

PETER LANG PUBLISHING, INC.
62 West 45th Street
USA – New York, NY 10036

Richard Wakefield

ROBERT FROST
and the Opposing Lights of the Hour

American University Studies: Series IV (English Language and Literature).
Vol. 16
ISBN 0-8204-0152-8   222 pages   hardback US $ 27.70 / sFr. 63.70

Recommended prices – alterations reserved

Robert Frost's early poems establish a philosophy that became, in his later work, more explicit but seldom more powerfully expressed. He believed that activity has meaning only when it is an exertion against opposition, that we establish ourselves, virtually create ourselves, in the range of movement allowed us by external constraints. Speech, as activity, likewise takes on character when placed in opposition to the mechanical rhythms of poetry – and thus for Frost did a philosophy of life cohere with a theory of poetry.

Contents: Voice against rhythm – Self against nature – Self against society – Self-preservation against the re-definition of romantic love – The necessity of discovering the range in which meaningful activity can take place.

PETER LANG PUBLISHING, INC.
62 West 45th Street
USA – New York, NY 10036